AN ILLUSTRATED GUIDE TO

RIFLES

AND SUB-MACHINE GUNS

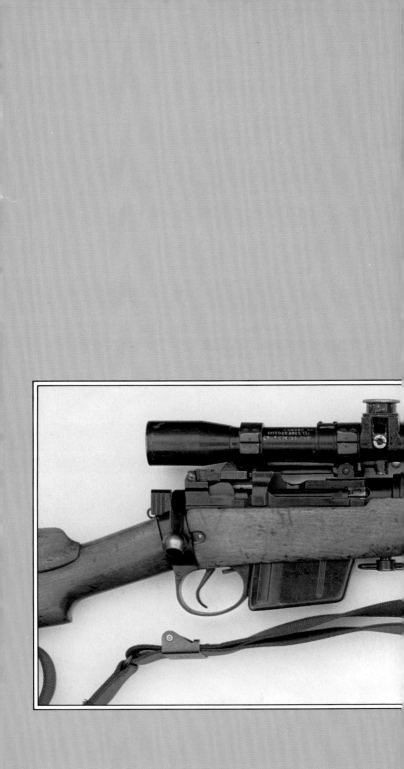

AN ILLUSTRATED GUIDE TO

RIFLES

AND SUB-MACHINE GUNS

Major Frederick Myatt M.C.

a Salamander book

Published by Salamander Books Limited
LONDON

A Salamander Book

© 1981 Salamander Books Ltd, Salamander House,
27 Old Gloucester Street, London WC1N 3AF, United Kingdom.

ISBN 0 86101 077 9

Distributed in the United Kingdom by New English Library Ltd.

All rights reserved. No part of this book may be reproduced,
stored in a retrieval system or transmitted in any form or by any
means, electronic, mechanical, photocopying, recording or
otherwise, without the prior permission of Salamander Books Ltd.

All correspondence concerning the content of this volume should
be addressed to Salamander Books Ltd.

Publisher's note: The material in this book has previously
appeared in *Modern Small Arms.*

Contents

Rifles and automatic weapons are arranged in two groups, chronologically
within order of countries of origin.

RIFLES AND CARBINES

Author: Major Frederick Myatt, M.C., is Curator of the Weapons Museum, School of Infantry, Warminster. Among his many books on military subjects are the Salamander titles *19th Century Firearms* and *Pistols and Revolvers*.

Consultant: Colonel John Weeks, internationally recognised expert on weaponry and author of several books on military subjects.

Editor: Richard O'Neill
Designer: Barry Savage
Photography of weapons: Bruce Scott © Salamander Books Ltd.
Photographs: A full list of credits is given on page 158.
Filmset: Modern Text Ltd. England.
Colour reproduction: Tempus Litho Ltd. England.
Printed by: Henri Proost et Cie. Turnhout. Belgium.

The Rifle and Carbine

American soldiers in training with M16A1 (Armalite AR-15) rifles.
Note the blank-firing adaptors attached to the rifles' muzzles.

Rifled firearms, in which slow, spiral, parallel grooves cut into the bore impart spin to the projectile and give it a considerable degree of stability in flight, existed as early as the 16th century. They were, however, both expensive to make and very slow to load, since a tight-fitting lead sphere had to be forced down the full length of the barrel from the muzzle end. Thus, the rifle remained for many years a weapon mainly for wealthy sportsmen and game shooters.

It is thought that a few rifles, then called "screwed guns", were used as sniper-type arms during the English Civil Wars (1642-51), but probably the first to make wide use of rifled arms were the frontiersmen of North America, who relied on game-shooting

for food and other necessities. There evolved a characteristic "long rifle", with a barrel length of up to 4ft (1299mm) and a calibre of around 0·5in (12mm). Reloading was speeded up by wrapping the ball in a circular patch of oiled leather or linen.

During the 18th century, the American colonists' rifles proved their worth against Red Indians; against the French in the Seven Years' War (1756-63); and against British regulars during the American Revolution of 1775-83 — when the British also made effective use of the Ferguson breechloading rifle.

Rifles in 19th-Century Warfare

The rifle's value as a specialist arm was apparent to many British officers who had served in America — and the French use of skirmishers to precede their attacking columns during the Revolutionary Wars necessitated the use of similar troops in opposition. In 1800, therefore, the British Army raised a Rifle Regiment armed with the Baker flintlock, which shot fairly well to 300yds (274m). In the 1850s, reloading speed was much improved by the adoption, first, of the French-developed Minié rifle — taking an elongated projectile with a hollow base, which expanded the lead bullet into the rifling *after* it had been rammed down — and then of the Enfield rifle.

The Enfield, although still loading at only about two rounds per minute, shot well to c880yds (805m) in expert hands, dramatically increasing the effective fire zone of infantry in defence. Most of the world's modern armies were soon equipped with similar weapons. Their effect on tactics, evident in the American Civil War

An American soldier fires his ·30 Calibre M1 (Garand) rifle;
the PFC in the foreground has a Browning Automatic Rifle (BAR).

(1861-65), was profound: battles became more open and started at greater ranges; frontal attacks became suicidal; defensive works, ie, trenches, were essential; and the roles of cavalry and horse artillery were radically changed and limited.

But most European powers clung to their percussion muzzle-loaders in spite of the obvious need for effective breechloaders. Although Prussia developed the "needle-gun" — a single shot, bolt-action rifle firing a non-metallic consumable cartridge — in the 1840s, the arm was not widely taken up. Nevertheless, Prussian victories over the Danes (1864), the Austrians (1866) and the French (in 1870; when the French Army had a superior needle-gun type, the Chassepot, but failed to derive a tactical advantage), led to general acceptance of the single-shot, bolt-action rifle firing self-contained cartridges. Rate of fire was increased by such devices as the Snider hinged-block breech — the Martini-Henry falling-block breech rifle was in general British issue by c1874 — but these were soon superseded by rifles with tubular or box magazines, using smokeless powder.

The 5·56mm Galil assault rifle, seen here with grenade-firing attachment, has been in service with Israeli forces since 1972.

Russian soldiers armed with 7·62mm Mosin-Nagant rifles in the trenches during World War I.

The French Army's recently adopted 5·56mm FA MAS rifle is fired from its bipod.

The 20th Century: Automatic Weapons

The power of the modern magazine rifle was demonstrated at its peak by the British Expeditionary Force of 1914, which, with the short-magazine Lee-Enfield, repeatedly halted German attacks with rifle fire of unprecedented speed, accuracy and intensity. But during World War I the demands of trench warfare brought forward other weapons which tended to overshadow the rifle. Although it remained the standard infantry arm, it never regained its former supremacy.

Most countries entered World War II with rifles similar in type and capacity to the British Number 4. The Germans mainly used the KAR 98K, a shortened version of the reliable Gewehr 98; the French had the MAS 36; the Russians the M1891/30. Only the Americans were fully equipped with a self-loading rifle, the ·300 M1 (Garand), with a similar carbine firing a much lighter cartridge. The Germans experimented with self-loaders in 1941-43 without great success, and such weapons did not become general until post-War.

World War II saw the rise in importance of the sub-machine gun (see pages 80-157): in the infantry, a number of these were interspersed among the rifles. It became clear that, with a vast number of support weapons, the need for a long-range rifle was much reduced. Thus, attempts were made at an intermediate weapon—a "hotted-up" sub-machine gun—to fill both roles. The first of these arms, later called assault rifles, was the German FG 42, an excellent weapon firing the standard rifle cartridge, which was followed by the equally efficient MG 44, firing a round

intermediate between the 9mm pistol and the rifle cartridge. Russia's post-War AK 47 was closely based on the German rifle; the US developed the Colt Armalite range; and many countries followed suit. Great Britain experimented with the satisfactory EM 2, but did not adopt it; she is now testing a small-bore assault weapon of broadly similar type — the 4·85mm Individual Weapon — with a heavy-barrelled version capable of acting as the section automatic weapon. An earlier British development worthy of note is the 5·56mm Sterling-Armalite AR-18 rifle. This is a version of the Armalite AR-15 — the US Army's standard M16 rifle — specially designed to be simple and cheap to make. Mechanically similar to the AR-15, it is simplified to obviate the use of specialised tooling in its manufacture: the body is made of a single sheet of steel, welding is extensively used, and all its furniture is of fibreglass.

A current arm that has something in common with Britain's abandoned EM 2 is the 5·56mm FA MAS, which was accepted as its standard rifle by the French Army in the late 1970s. It has also been submitted for NATO trials, with the claim that it can be adapted to fire any small-calibre round. Fed by a 25-round box magazine, and with a cyclic rate of 900-1000 rpm, it is capable of fully- or semi-automatic fire, or three-round bursts, and may be fired from either shoulder or from a bipod to an effective range of c330yds (300m). At the muzzle is an attachment to permit the firing of 22mm tubed anti-tank or anti-personnel grenades. Its distinctive outline, with a large, over-arching carrying handle, has won it the French nickname of *Clarion* ("Bugle"). Also currently in

Above: *Soviet infantryman fires the 7·62mm AKM assault rifle, a modernisation of the AK 47, in production since 1959. Note the small recess in the side of the receiver, directly over the magazine, and the small muzzle compensator: both are among the features that distinguish it from the AK 47.*

Right: *An American mortarman is preceded by infantry armed with ·30 Calibre M1 (Garand) rifles and M1 carbines as they advance cautiously through ruined houses at St Malo, 1944.*

Far right: *The soldier of the Laotian People's Liberation Army standing atop the armoured car is armed with a Chinese Type 56 rifle, a close copy of the Soviet AK 47 assault rifle.*

service is the Belgian 5·56mm FN CAL rifle. This was one of the earlier small-calibre rifles developed in Europe, appearing in 1966. Although its designation is *Carabine Automatique Légère* (ie, light automatic carbine), it is considered an assault rifle.

Assault Rifles in Service

Among the most notable assault rifles currently in service (other than those illustrated on the colour pages of this book) are the 5·56mm Galil, adopted by the Israeli Defence Forces in 1972; the Soviet 7·62mm AKM, an updated version of the AK 47 (see page 62), in general use among Warsaw Pact countries and in some Arab armies since the early 1960s; the Soviet 5·45mm AKS 74; and the Chinese 7·62mm Type 68, an improved, longer-barrelled version of the Type 56 (see page 54).

The gas-operated, air-cooled Galil is a versatile arm with both
sub-machine gun (in a short-barrelled configuration) and light
machine gun capabilities. As an assault rifle/SMG it is fed from a
35-round box; a 12-round box is used for ballistite cartridges
when the arm is used as a grenade projector. As an LMG,
equipped with bipod, it is fed from a 50-round box and is capable
of aimed fire to c550yds (500m) at a maximum 650 rpm. It is
also made under licence in Sweden, where it has been under
consideration by the Swedish Army, as the FFV 890 C assault
rifle. Far less is known of the AKS 74, which was reported to be
coming into general service with Soviet forces in the late 1970s. It
is believed that this small-calibre member of the AK family may
fire a very high-velocity round superior to the very similar
ammunition of the West's M16A1 (see page 76).

New arms of small-calibre type have many advantages, including lightness and portability, which are important in the close confines of the various armoured personnel carriers in which the infantryman now spends much of his time. Thus, it seems probable that in the future they will largely replace both the sub-machine gun and the more orthodox rifle. The only exception is likely to be the retention of the older bolt-action rifle fitted with a telescopic sight in the role of a sniping rifle, a function which it performed well in both World Wars and in various later operations.

Effective Ranges

A brief note on the ranges of rifles is necessary, since maximum backsight settings — as given in the data tables — may be misleading. The original late-19th century, small-bore, bolt-action, magazine rifles were usually sighted to c2000yds (1829m) and sometimes had auxiliary long-range sights to 2800yds (2650m). Under ideal conditions, fire could be directed to these extreme ranges, in the sense that thirty or so men firing together could bring collective fire to bear on an area target. Such fire was marginally effective at best.

All things being equal, fire effect increased as range shortened so that at c800yds (730m) well-controlled collective fire could be deadly: at Omdurman, in 1898, tribesmen charging across open ground rarely got within 400yds (366m) of the British firing line, and then at terrible cost. In South Africa, around the turn of the century, Boer riflemen shot well to c1000yds (914m) and were not usually much worried by British long-range collective volley fire in return. But the South African experience was atypical: the mass infantry tactics of the Russo-Japanese War were a better pointer to the way in which modern warfare would develop. Thus, by 1914, the British at least had decided that the real answer was rapid fire at effective ranges—which, with regard to the very high standard of British musketry, meant up to 500yds (475m).

Thereafter, automatic weapons largely took over the task of delivering greater volumes of fire, and the effective range of the rifle was reduced accordingly. Most modern rifles are still sighted to c800yds (730m), but they are rarely used above 300yds (274m), which may therefore be considered the maximum truly effective range by modern standards. The same is broadly true of the effective range of light machine guns.

Above: *A soldier of General J.P. Koenig's Free French light division, which held the Bir Hacheim position in the Western Desert from February to June 1942, displays the banner of the Foreign Legion on the bayonet of his 7·5mm Fusil MAS 36.*

Left: *Soldiers of the People's Republic of China, wearing respirators and mounted on a K-63 APC, fire their 7·62mm Type 68 assault rifles. Note the characteristic folding bayonet and the knurled, two-position gas regulator. This Chinese-designed and manufactured arm closely resembles the Type 56, but with a longer barrel, and is normally fed from a 15-round box magazine.*

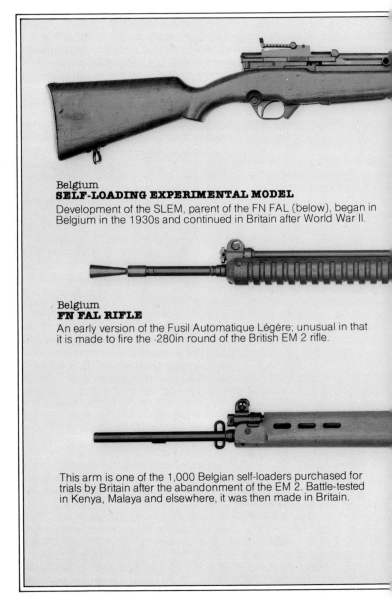

Belgium
SELF-LOADING EXPERIMENTAL MODEL
Development of the SLEM, parent of the FN FAL (below), began in Belgium in the 1930s and continued in Britain after World War II.

Belgium
FN FAL RIFLE
An early version of the Fusil Automatique Légère; unusual in that it is made to fire the ·280in round of the British EM 2 rifle.

This arm is one of the 1,000 Belgian self-loaders purchased for trials by Britain after the abandonment of the EM 2. Battle-tested in Kenya, Malaya and elsewhere, it was then made in Britain.

SELF-LOADING EXPERIMENTAL MODEL

Length:	44" (1117mm)
Weight:	9·5lb (4·31kg)
Barrel:	23·25" (591mm)
Calibre:	7·92mm
Rifling:	4 groove r/hand
Operation:	Gas
Feed:	10-round box
Muz Vel:	2400 f/s (730 m/s)
Sights:	1094 yds (1000m)

FN FAL RIFLE

Length:	41·5" (1054mm)
Weight:	9·5lb (4·31kg)
Barrel:	21" (533mm)
Calibre:	7·62mm
Rifling:	4 groove r/hand
Operation:	Gas
Feed:	20-round box
Muz Vel:	2800 f/s (853 m/s)
Sights:	656 yds (600m)

7·92mm Patrone 98
·280" Experimental
7·62mm NATO

·303" SAA Ball

Belgium
SELF-LOADING
EXPERIMENTAL MODEL

This weapon was originally designed in Belgium in the 1930s by a M. Saive, who envisaged it as a replacement for the existing bolt-action rifles of Mauser type then in use in the Belgian Army. In May 1940, however, soon after the outbreak of World War II the Germans invaded Belgium and all work on the new rifle naturally stopped. The designer managed to escape from Belgium with the plans for his new weapon which he took with him to Britain.

Saive, like other refugees, continued to work for Great Britain on various wartime projects but nothing was done about his own rifle until the end of the war when a number were made at the Royal Small Arms Factory at Enfield, being generally known as the Self-Loading Experimental Model, often abbreviated to SLEM. They were gas operated with a gas cylinder above the barrel, and had a bolt very similar to that of the Russian Tokarev rifle. They were in general well made and full-stocked in walnut which made them very expensive weapons to produce. These prototypes, which were all made to fire the full size German 7·92mm Mauser round, were extensively tested, but although they proved to be most successful the British were then also carrying out tests on their own EM 2, and so they took no further action on the Belgian rifle. When M. Saive returned to Belgium, however, he continued his work there and soon perfected an improved model known usually as the Model 49, after the date of its appearance. This was a time when a good many countries were looking for cheap and reliable self-loaders with which to re-arm their infantry, and the Model 49 was an immediate success, being sold to a considerable number of countries including Columbia, Venezuela, Egypt and Luxemburg. The Belgians, understandably anxious for business, were more than ready to produce what their customers wanted and the Model 49 was manufactured in a variety of calibres. The Belgian Army also adopted it and it saw service in Korea. It subsequently developed into the highly successful FAL.

Belgium
FN FAL RIFLE

The Belgians, who have long been well known as arms makers, had made considerable progress in developing a self-loading rifle before the war. The designer escaped to Britain with the plans for this weapon which was later made in England and which subsequently formed the basis of all future Belgian

development. Full details of this early weapon are given at the top of this page. The FAL (Fusil Automatique Légère) first appeared in 1950; it was originally intended to fire the German intermediate round, but was subsequently altered to fire the standard NATO cartridge, after which it very soon became popular. It was gas-operated, could fire automatic or single shots as required, and was generally a robust and effective arm well suited to military needs, and sold to a great many countries. Although it had the capacity to fire bursts this led to problems of accuracy due to the inevitable tendency of the muzzle to rise, and most countries therefore had their rifles permanently set at semi-automatic which still allowed twenty or thirty well-aimed shots to be fired in one minute. There was also a heavy barrelled version with a light bipod which some countries adopted as a section automatic. There have been many modifications in design to suit the particular needs of different purchasers, but most of these are relatively minor ones. When Great Britain abandoned her EM 2 she decided, like many other countries, to adopt a version of the Belgian self-loader and purchased one thousand of them for trials, the lower weapon illustrated being one of these originals. As usual some modifications were incorporated and the weapon was fairly extensively tested under operational conditions in Kenya, Malaya, and elsewhere before being taken into use, after which it was made in England. The upper of the two rifles illustrated is a very early version of the Fusil Automatique Légère rifle made to fire the ·280" round originally designed for the British EM2 rifle. The object of this is not known, but presumably if the British rifle had been accepted some countries might have preferred a more orthodox looking weapon but in the same calibre as the British EM 2.

NATO troops on the firing line with FN FAL rifles. This Belgian arm first appeared in 1950 and was adopted by over 70 countries.

MODEL VZ 52

Length:	40" (1016mm)
Weight:	9lb (4·08kg)
Barrel:	20·5" (521mm)
Calibre:	7·62mm
Rifling:	4 groove r/hand
Operation:	Gas
Feed:	10-round box
Muz Vel:	2440 f/s (740 m/s)
Sights:	984 yds (900m)

Czechoslovakia
MODEL VZ 52

France
MODELE 1886 (LEBEL)

France
FUSIL MAS 36

MODELE 1886 (LEBEL)

Length:	51" (1295mm)
Weight:	9·3lb (4·22kg)
Barrel:	31·5" (800mm)
Calibre:	8mm
Rifling:	4 groove l/hand
Operation:	Bolt
Feed:	8-round tubular
Muz Vel:	2350 f/s (716 m/s)
Sights:	2187 yds (2000m)

FUSIL MAS 36

Length:	40·15" (1020mm)
Weight:	8·31 (3·76kg)
Barrel:	22·6" (574mm)
Calibre:	7·5mm
Rifling:	4 groove l/hand
Operation:	Bolt
Feed:	5-round box
Muz Vel:	2700 f/s (823 m/s)
Sights:	1312 yds (1200m)

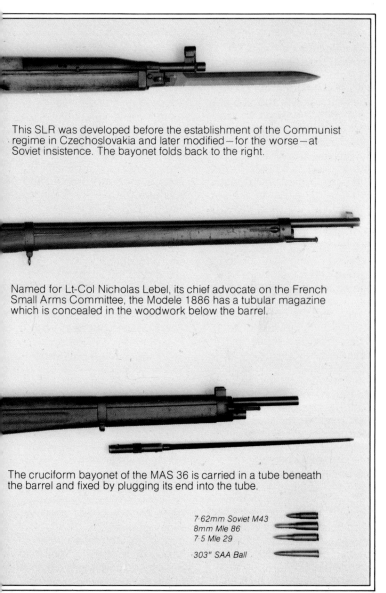

This SLR was developed before the establishment of the Communist regime in Czechoslovakia and later modified—for the worse—at Soviet insistence. The bayonet folds back to the right.

Named for Lt-Col Nicholas Lebel, its chief advocate on the French Small Arms Committee, the Modele 1886 has a tubular magazine which is concealed in the woodwork below the barrel.

The cruciform bayonet of the MAS 36 is carried in a tube beneath the barrel and fixed by plugging its end into the tube.

7·62mm Soviet M43
8mm Mle 86
7·5 Mle 29

·303" SAA Ball

MODEL VZ 52

This self-loading rifle was designed and developed in Czechoslovakia towards the end of World War II, some time before the country was swept into the Communist bloc. It incorporates a considerable variety of ideas borrowed from earlier arms of similar type. It was originally designed to fire an inter-mediate-type cartridge of purely Czech design and not interchangeable with any other, and was gas-operated. The method actually adopted how-ever was somewhat unusual in that the weapon had no gas cylinder or piston of the usual type, power being transmitted by a sleeve round the barrel which was forced sharply to the rear by the pressure of the gas tapped off from the bore and taking the bolt with it. The bolt was rather unusual in that it worked on the tilting principle under which the front end of the bolt dropped into a recess cut into the bottom of the body which had the effect of locking it firmly at the instant of firing. The rifle performed well with the original cartridge for which it was designed, but the Russians later compelled the Czechs to abandon that round in favour of their own less powerful version which adversely affected its performance even though it helped standardization. The new modified rifle was generally known as the Model 52/57. The original VZ 52 was relatively heavy which reduced recoil but added to the soldier's load. It lacked any simple system of gas regulation, so that any change involved the removal of the foregrip before the gas stop could be adjusted,

and then only on a trial and error basis which would have made it inconvenient in service. It was often stocked in poor quality wood of a dusty yellow colour and had a generally cheap and clumsy look about it. It was fitted with a permanently attached blade bayonet which folded back along the right-hand side of the body when not in use. Both the VZ 52 and the VZ 52/57 are now deemed to be obsolete.

France
MODELE 1886 (LEBEL)

The first breechloading rifle adopted by France was the Modèle 1866 or Chassepot, a bolt action needle-fire weapon firing a consumable paper cartridge. It was similar to the Prussian needle-gun, although of superior performance, and was used by the French in the war of 1870-71. It was converted to fire a modern metallic cartridge in 1873 and replaced by the Gras, a very similar weapon, in 1874. Four years later the French Marine Infantry was rearmed with the Austrian Kropatschek rifle, and it was on this weapon that the new Modèle 1886 was based. The Modèle 1886 was probably much better known as the Lebel, the name being in honour of Lieutenant-Colonel Nicholas Lebel, a member of the French Small Arms Committee at the time and the officer chiefly responsible for its introduction. It was a bolt-action rifle which incor-porated the somewhat unusual feature of a tubular magazine, concealed in the woodwork below the barrel, in place of the more general box. This type of magazine, which had been largely developed by the United States, had also been a feature of the earlier French Marine rifle. It incorporated a powerful coil spring at its front end, the rear end of the spring being fitted with a close fitting plug, and the rifle was loaded by pushing the rounds nose first into the magazine opening below the chamber until the full capacity of eight had been reached. The contents of the magazine could if necessary be kept in reserve by a cut-off device, allowing the rifle to be used as a single-loader until a more rapid burst of fire was required. The most important feature of the Lebel was undoubtedly the fact that its cartridges were loaded with a recently developed smokeless propellant instead of the old black powder, the French being the first to make this important change. Smokeless powder had two obvious advantages, in that the firing line could be easily concealed while the target was never obscured by smoke as had often been the case with black powder. In order to get the maximum power from the cartridge, it was made bottle shaped instead of cylindrical so as to get as much propellant in as possible. Smokeless powder cartridges soon came into general use, but in view of the greater pressures which developed, older pattern rifles could not always be adapted and new arms were vital.

France
FUSIL MAS 36

By the end of World War I it was clear to the French that they required a new rifle cartridge. The original Lebel smokeless round of 1886 had been revolutionary in its day but inevitably more modern rounds had been developed since. Its real disadvantage was its shape, since its very wide base and sharp taper made it a very difficult cartridge to use in automatic weapons. As by 1918 these dominated the battlefield a change was necessary. In 1924 therefore, a new rimless cartridge was developed, based fairly closely on the German 7·92mm round. The first priority was to develop suitable automatic weapons which are described elsewhere in this book, but once this was complete a new rifle was also put into production. MAS 36 was a bolt action rifle of modified Mauser type, but with the bolt designed to lock into the top of the body behind the magazine. This made it necessary to angle the bolt lever forward so as to be in reach of the firer's hand, the general effect being rather ugly. The magazine was of standard integral box type with a capacity of five rounds and there was no manual safety catch. The rifle had a cruciform bayonet carried in a tube beneath the barrel. It was fixed by withdrawing it and plugging its cylindrical handle into the mouth of the tube where it was held in place by a spring. Small numbers of a modified MAS 36 were later made for airborne troops; they had shorter barrels and folding butts and were designated the MAS 36 CR39.

Suez, 1956: the French paratrooper in the foreground is armed with a Fusil MAS 36.

GEWEHR 98

Length:	49·25" (1250mm)
Weight:	9lb (4·1kg)
Barrel:	29·25" (740mm)
Calibre:	7·92mm
Rifling:	4 groove r/hand
Operation:	Bolt
Feed:	5-round box
Muz Vel:	2850 f/s (870 m/s)
Sights:	2188 yds (2000m)

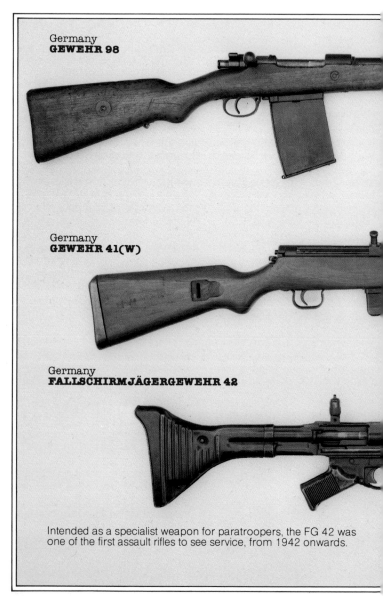

Germany
GEWEHR 98

Germany
GEWEHR 41(W)

Germany
FALLSCHIRMJÄGERGEWEHR 42

Intended as a specialist weapon for paratroopers, the FG 42 was one of the first assault rifles to see service, from 1942 onwards.

GEWEHR 41(W)

Length:	44·5" (1130mm)
Weight:	11lb (4·98kg)
Barrel:	21·5" (546mm)
Calibre:	7·92mm
Rifling:	4 groove r/hand
Operation:	Gas
Feed:	10-round box
Muz Vel:	2550 f/s (776 m/s)
Sights:	1313 yds (1200m)

FALLSCHIRM-JÄGERGEWEHR 42

Length:	37" (940mm)
Weight:	9·95lb (4·5kg)
Barrel:	20" (508mm)
Calibre:	7·92mm Patrone 98
Rifling:	4 groove r/hand
Operation:	Gas
Feed:	20-round box
Muz Vel:	2500 f/s (762 m/s)
Sights:	1313 yds (1200m)

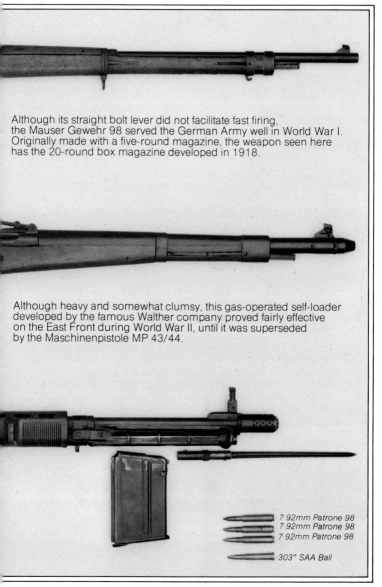

Although its straight bolt lever did not facilitate fast firing,
the Mauser Gewehr 98 served the German Army well in World War I.
Originally made with a five-round magazine, the weapon seen here
has the 20-round box magazine developed in 1918.

Although heavy and somewhat clumsy, this gas-operated self-loader
developed by the famous Walther company proved fairly effective
on the East Front during World War II, until it was superseded
by the Maschinenpistole MP 43/44.

7·92mm Patrone 98
7·92mm Patrone 98
7·92mm Patrone 98

·303" SAA Ball

Germany
GEWEHR 98

The Germans were the first nation to adopt a bolt action rifle which they did as early as 1848 when their needle-gun officially came into service. Thereafter, unlike the British who went off at a tangent with hinged and falling block rifles, the Germans remained constant to this original system which they developed progressively. The first rifle to fire a smokeless round was introduced in 1888 and was of 7·92mm calibre; this was followed in 1898 by the model illustrated which was made by the well-known firm of Mauser. It was a strong and reliable arm with the forward locking lugs made famous by the makers, and a five-round magazine the bottom of which was flush with the stock, and although its straight bolt lever was clumsy and not well adapted to fast fire, this was a minor disadvantage which did nothing to detract from its popularity. In one form or another it was sold to a great number of different countries and there can have been few rifles produced in such large quantities. A considerable number of the earliest ones were bought by the Boers who used them with tremendous effect in their war with the British which broke out a year later, and it served the German Army well in World War I. In 1918 the Germans experimented with a twenty-round magazine to prevent the constant entry of mud from the continuous reloading inseparable from the five-round magazine, but this was not a success chiefly because a spring powerful enough to lift such a column of cartridges made manual operation difficult.

Germany
GEWEHR 41(W)

The Germans were among the pioneers of self-loading rifles and had a complete regiment armed with weapons of this type as early as 1901. This experiment was not followed up, principally because although valuable information was obtained the rifle then used was too heavy for an individual weapon. A few weapons of this type were used in World War I, but the main pre-occupation in 1914-18 was with a great volume of fire from somewhat heavier automatic weapons so again no progress was made. It was not therefore until the appearance of the Russian Tokarev self-loader just before World War II that any real attention was paid to the subject and by 1941 two separate models were undergoing tests. The first was the 41 (Mauser) which incorporated a bolt similar to that of the manually operated rifle; it was never a success and was soon abandoned. The second was the 41 (Walther) and this was a good deal more successful. It incorporated a muzzle cap which deflected part of the gases back onto an annular piston that worked a rod placed above the barrel, its return spring however being below it. This piston rod worked the bolt and the concept was reasonably satisfactory, although the arm had certain defects notably its weight and balance, together with a serious tendency to foul very badly round the muzzle cap. It was manufactured in some quantity and issued chiefly to units on the Russian front. It was eventually replaced by the MP 43/44, a much superior weapon.

A German soldier armed with a 7·92mm Gewehr 98 rifle seeks cover during action.

German soldier with Gewehr 41 rifle slung guards Polish PoWs taken in the fighting of 1939.

Germany
FALLSCHIRM-JÄGERGEWEHR 42

This was one of the earliest assault rifles, being introduced in 1942. Its main disadvantage was that although the Germans had gained some success with intermediate cartridges, this particular arm fired the full-sized rifle round which was really too powerful for it. In spite of this it proved to be a remarkably good weapon to the limited number of troops armed with it, most of whom were parachutists. It was capable of single rounds or bursts. When bursts were employed the FG 42 fired from an open bolt, that is, there was no round in the chamber until the bolt drove one in and fired it in the same movement; the reason for this was that the chamber tended to get sufficiently hot to fire a cartridge left in it even for a very short time. It would take a bayonet and was equipped with a light bipod. Unfortunately it was expensive to make and being something of a specialist weapon for paratroops, its use declined during the war.

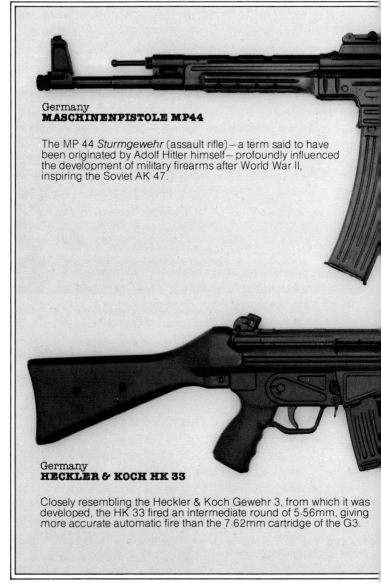

Germany
MASCHINENPISTOLE MP44

The MP 44 *Sturmgewehr* (assault rifle)—a term said to have been originated by Adolf Hitler himself—profoundly influenced the development of military firearms after World War II, inspiring the Soviet AK 47.

Germany
HECKLER & KOCH HK 33

Closely resembling the Heckler & Koch Gewehr 3, from which it was developed, the HK 33 fired an intermediate round of 5·56mm, giving more accurate automatic fire than the 7·62mm cartridge of the G3.

MASCHINENPISTOLE MP44

Length:	37" (940mm)
Weight:	11·25lb (5·1kg)
Barrel:	16·5" (420mm)
Calibre:	7·92mm
Rifling:	4 groove r/hand
Feed:	30-round box
Muz Vel:	2125 f/s (647 m/s)
C. Rate:	500 rpm
Sights:	875 yds (800m)

HECKLER & KOCH HK 33

Length:	37" (940mm)
Weight:	7·7lb (3·5kg)
Barrel:	15" (382mm)
Calibre:	5·56mm
Rifling:	6 groove r/hand
Feed:	20-, 30-, 40-round box
Muz Vel:	3145 f/s (960 m/s)
C. Rate:	600 rpm
Sights:	437·5 yds (400m)

7·92mm Kurz
5·56mm × 45mm
·303" SAA Ball

Germany
MASCHINENPISTOLE MP44

The experience of World War I led the Germans to the opinion that in the future the infantryman should have a lighter weapon than the standard rifle. Work on this project started before the war and by 1941 they had produced an efficient intermediate round suitable for a weapon of the kind proposed. Perhaps surprisingly this round does not seem to have been considered for the FG 42, which was being developed at that time but which fired the standard rifle round. Instead a number of weapons were developed for it, and by 1942 these had been whittled down to two, one by Haenel, the other by Walther, both being described as machine carbines. The Haenel version was modified by Schmeisser in 1943 in the light of actual combat experience, after which it became the MP 43, the Walther alternative being dropped at the same time. The new weapon, which was gas operated through a piston working in a gas cylinder above the barrel, was an immediate success and by the end of 1943 the German Army had received fourteen thousand of them. The long-term idea seems to have been to make the MP 43 a universal weapon at squad or section level, so doing away with rifles, sub-machine guns and light machine guns in favour of the new arm. Perhaps fortunately, production declined very rapidly after the first few months of 1944 and so the new concept was never realized. There were some variations to the standard type, notably an MP 43 (1) which

had a fixture allowing it to fire grenades, but no really significant changes. In 1944 the designation was changed to MP 44, apparently to mark the change in year since no other reason was ever offered, and by the end of the same year the weapon had been given the additional title of Sturm-Gewehr, or Assault Rifle. It is said that the expression was coined by Hitler himself; whether this is true or not it was a very apt description and one which has been used ever since. The MP 44 had a profound effect on the development of infantry firearms; the Russians in particular were quick to see the advantages of this new type of arm and very soon developed their own version in the shape of the AK 47

Germany
HECKLER & KOCH HK 33

This weapon has a long and somewhat involved history. It had its origins in a German rifle designed in the course of World War II. After the war this rifle was largely redesigned by a number of German designers

and engineers who were working in Spain; the resulting weapon being the Spanish CETME. When the German Army was reformed in the 1950s the German firm of Heckler-Koch, which had been involved with the CETME, developed the design somewhat further and produced a rifle known as the Gewehr 3. This soon became the weapon of the German Army and is, or has been, extensively used by a considerable number of other countries, some of whom bought them from Heckler-Koch while others made them themselves under licence. The G3 was of somewhat unusual design in that it worked not on gas (by far the most common method) but on delayed blowback. The breech was never fully locked in the strict sense of the word; it was equipped with rollers which the forward movement of the firing pin forced outwards into recesses in the receiver. The shape of these recesses and their relationship to the rollers was such that the breech was

held closed until the pressure dropped to a safe level when the rollers were forced out of the recesses. The residual gas pressure in the chamber blew the empty case backwards, taking the bolt with it and compressing the return spring which caused the cycle to be repeated. This method proved to be successful although the use of a full-sized rifle cartridge does often cause problems in a breech of this nature. The main difficulty is that the bolt comes back fairly fast, with no preliminary turning motion to start the case, and this can cause problems of extraction; this was basically the problem of the American Pedersen rifle which is dealt with elsewhere in this section. In the G3 the problem was dealt with by fluting the chamber and by ensuring that the quality of brass used in the case was sufficient to withstand the initial jerk without having its base torn off. The HK 33 was simply a logical development of this earlier weapon, to which it bears a strong resemblance both externally and mechanically. The chief, and important difference is that the HK 33 was designed to fire an intermediate round which offered some advantages. It gave good performance at reasonable ranges and allowed for much more accurate automatic fire than was ever the case with the more powerful 7·62mm cartridge.

The HK 33 is no longer made but there are several derivations from it, including some with telescopic butts, a sniper model, and a shortened version.

German Maschinenpistole MP44 fitted with Krummlauf *attachment. With the aid of a periscope, the user was able to fire at angles of 30-90°.*

Great Britain
SHORT MAGAZINE LEE-ENFIELD MARKS III AND V

Great Britain
PATTERN 1913 RIFLE

SHORT MAGAZINE LEE-ENFIELD MARKS III AND V		PATTERN 1913 RIFLE	
Length:	44·5" (1130mm)	**Length:**	46·3" (1176m)
Weight:	8·2lb (3·71kg)	**Weight:**	8·7lb (3·94kg)
Barrel:	25" (635mm)	**Barrel:**	26" (661mm)
Calibre:	·303"	**Calibre:**	·276"
Rifling:	5 groove l/hand	**Rifling:**	5 groove l/hand
Operation:	Bolt	**Operation:**	Bolt
Feed:	10-round box	**Feed:**	5-round box
Muz Vel:	2440 f/s (738 m/s)	**Muz Vel:**	2785 f/s (843 m/s)
Sights:	2000 yds (1829m)	**Sights:**	1900 yds (1738m)

Upper: The SMLE Mark III, with its 18in (457mm) sword bayonet, equipped the British Army during World War I.

Lower: The SMLE Mark V, which first appeared in 1923, differs from the Mark III principally in having an aperture backsight in place of the open U-type sight of earlier Lee-Enfields.

Advocates of the forward-locking Mauser system were largely responsible for the development of the Pattern 1913 rifle: a disastrous design—slow to fire, noisy, and prone to excessive fouling in the barrel and over-heating at the breech.

·303" SAA Ball
·303" SAA Ball
·276" Experimental
·303" SAA Ball

Men of the 1st Cameron Highlanders, armed with Short Magazine Lee-Enfield rifles (apparently Mark IIIs) at Cuinchy, April 1918.

Great Britain
SHORT MAGAZINE LEE-ENFIELD MARKS III AND V

British experience in the South African war of 1899-1902 showed the need for a short rifle for universal use and even before the end of the war a new weapon had been produced and a thousand made for trials. It was also tested operationally in the fighting against the Mad Mullah in Somaliland, and after some modification emerged as the Short Magazine Lee-Enfield Mark II in 1907. It was an excellent weapon and although slightly less accurate than its predecessor it had certain compensating advantages, notably its easy breech mechanism which allowed a fast rate of manipulation. The British Army had concentrated on rapid rifle fire to the stage where every soldier could fire at least fifteen well-aimed shots in a minute, and the devastating effects of this were clearly seen

in the first few months of World War I when the gallant German infantry suffered heavily. The Mark III was a complex weapon to make, and in 1916 various simplifications were introduced, notably the abolition of the magazine cut-off and the disappearance of the special long-range collective fire sight which was clearly unnecessary in the age of the machine gun. These changed its designation to the Mark III*, perhaps the most famous rifle in British military history. It remained an excellent weapon with an eighteen inch sword bayonet for close quarter work and the ability to project grenades, either rodded or from a screw-on cup. Soon after the end of the war the British began to consider a new rifle, similar to its predecessor but easier to make by modern mass-production methods. The first step in this direction resulted in a new Mark V rifle which appeared in small numbers as early as 1923. Apart from an extra barrel band near the muzzle its main difference was that it had an aperture backsight rather than the open U-type of the earlier rifles, experience having shown that this type of sight was easier to teach, while the increased distance between backsight and foresight reduced the margin of error and made for more accurate shooting. In the end, however, it was decided that the conversion of the large existing stocks of rifles would be too expensive and although the development of a new rifle was maintained the British Army continued to rely on its well-tried Lee-Enfield until well after the outbreak of war in 1939. No separate data is given for the Mark V because apart from the fact that it was only sighted to 1400 yards it differed little from its predecessor.

Great Britain
PATTERN 1913 RIFLE

Although the Lee-Enfield series of rifle had proved remarkably successful there was still some residual prejudice against its bolt in favour of the forward locking Mauser sytem, and this seems to have been the main reason for the development of this new rifle. Work started on it in 1910 and by 1912 it was in limited production for troop trials which began the next year, hence the designation of the arm. Although of unmistakeable Enfield parentage it differed from the earlier range in that it had a Mauser-type bolt and fired a rimless cartridge from an integral five-round magazine. It also had an aperture backsight protected by a somewhat bulky extension on the body above the bolt way. It is perhaps not unfair to describe the Pattern 1913 as a near disaster, for although it

was very accurate there was little else to say for it. It was slow and clumsy to manipulate, particularly for men accustomed to the Lee-Enfield; it was subject to excessive metallic fouling in the bore; it had a tremendous flash and a correspondingly loud report; worst of all, the breech heated so fast that after fifteen rounds or so there was a distinct risk of the round firing as it went into the chamber, which was not conducive to good morale. Although extensive modifications were at once put in hand the project was finally shelved as far as the British Army was concerned by the outbreak of World War I which in view of the major role played by the British rifle in 1914 was probably just as well. Soon after the war started the rifle was converted to fire the standard British service round, but as there were no suitable facilities for making it in the United Kingdom arrangements were made to have it manufactured in the United States by the Winchester, Eddystone, and Remington factories.
This new rifle was then designated the Pattern 1914 and in view of its accuracy it was eventually used as a sniping rifle with the addition of a telescope sight. Apart from its different calibre its main external difference from its predecessor was in the absence of the inclined finger slots cut in the stock at the point of balance. The Pattern 1914 was also modified for use by the United States Army, by whom it was designated the Enfield 1917; large numbers of these were bought by Great Britain in 1940, mainly for the use of her Home Guard and the fact that they were of ·30″ calibre led to some confusion.

ROSS RIFLE MARK II

Length:	50·5" (1283mm)
Weight:	9·87lb (4·48kg)
Barrel:	30·15" (765mm)
Calibre:	·303"
Rifling:	4 groove l/hand
Operation:	Straight Pull
Feed:	5-round box
Muz Vel:	2600 f/s (794 m/s)
Sights:	1200 yds (1098m)

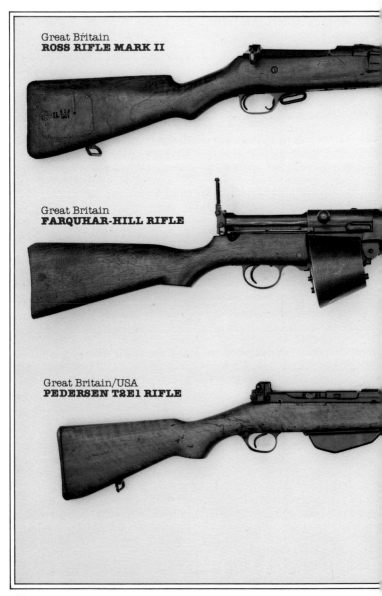

Great Britain
ROSS RIFLE MARK II

Great Britain
FARQUHAR-HILL RIFLE

Great Britain/USA
PEDERSEN T2E1 RIFLE

FARQUHAR-HILL RIFLE

Length:	41" (1042mm)
Weight:	14·5lb (6·58kg)
Barrel:	27" (686mm)
Calibre:	·303"
Rifling:	5 groove l/hand
Feed:	20-round drum
C. Rate:	6/700 rpm
Muz Vel:	2400 f/s (732 m/s)
Sights:	1500 yds (1372m)

PEDERSEN T2E1 RIFLE

Length:	45" (1143mm)
Weight:	9lb (4·1kg)
Barrel:	24" (610mm)
Calibre:	·276"
Rifling:	6 groove r/hand
Operation:	Blowback
Feed:	10-round box
Muz Vel:	2500 f/s (762 m/s)
Sights:	1200 yds (1098m)

This "straight-pull" rifle was issued to the Canadian Army in 1914, but soon proved to be unsatisfactory.

The third version of an automatic rifle designed before World War I. Note clockwork-powered magazine.

A British committee reported favourably on this rifle in 1932, but cartridge problems prevented adoption.

·303" SAA Ball
·303" SAA Ball
·276" Pedersen
·303" SAA Ball

At a sniper's post in the trenches at Hobb's Farm, near Houplines, in 1915, a subaltern of the 2nd Durham Light Infantry holds a Ross rifle. This rather unsatisfactory arm equipped the Canadian Army in 1914, but it was soon abandoned.

Great Britain
ROSS RIFLE MARK II

This rifle was designed by a Canadian, Sir Charles Ross, towards the end of the 19th Century, first issues being made in 1905 to the Royal Canadian Mounted Police. The rifle was unusual in being of the 'straight-pull' type in which the bolt handle was drawn straight back, the breech being unlocked by the rotation of the locking lugs by means of cams. It had a magazine capacity of five rounds which in the early models had to be loaded singly, and it proved to be an excellent target rifle. There were, however, fundamental defects in its design which rendered it unsuitable as a service rifle and although a whole series of modifications were hastily made there was no significant improvement. The British School of Musketry reported unfavourably on it but in spite of this the Canadian Army went to war with it in 1914, their particular weapon being the Mark III which could be loaded by charger. Its main fault, that the bolt stop bore on one of the locking lugs causing it to burr, led to disastrous consequences, particularly in the mud of the trenches when Canadian soldiers were seen angrily kicking their rifle bolts to open them during German attacks. It was quickly replaced by the Lee-Enfield and little more was heard of it although a few were resurrected for the British Home Guard in the early years of World War II.

Great Britain
FARQUHAR-HILL RIFLE

In 1908 a Major M. G. Farquhar produced an automatic rifle which he had invented in conjunction with Mr. Hill. There was at that time some military interest in automatic rifles and the weapon was tested by the Automatic Rifle Committee which the British Army had set up for the express purpose of investigating weapons of this type. The Farquhar-Hill, although well made by the Beardmore Company, turned out to be an extremely complex weapon. It utilized the system of long recoil, but faulty design kept the barrel and breech locked together long after the bullet had left the muzzle; this and other complications led to problems of feed and the gun was rejected. Nothing more was heard of it until 1917 when a second version appeared; this was described, very accurately, as a light machine gun with some potential as an aircraft gun, but was in fact an improved version of the earlier gun; its main difference was in its unusual magazine which was in the shape of a truncated cone, motive power being provided by a clockwork spring. This version was also tested and rejected, being very liable to fouling and prone to a variety of complex stoppages. It was in any case somewhat late, since it appeared at a time when the Lewis gun was giving good service. The inventors were extremely persistent and as late as 1924 they submitted the weapon illustrated. This had a similar but much smaller magazine with a capacity of ten rounds (as compared with up to sixty-five in the earlier versions) but again it was unsatisfactory (still mainly because of its defective magazine) and was not therefore adopted. Thus it passed into history.

Great Britain/USA
PEDERSEN T2E1 RIFLE

John Pedersen was a well-known designer of firearms in the United States, one of his best known inventions being a device to convert the standard Springfield rifle into a sub-machine gun in 1918. Between the wars he designed a self-loading rifle, together with a special cartridge for it, which attracted favourable attention in America. This new weapon also came to the notice of Messrs Vickers who manufactured a number under licence in England. The Pedersen was unusual in that its breech was not positively locked at the moment of discharge. Instead it made use of a hesitation-type lock, similar in principle to that of the Luger pistol but so designed that its various bearing surfaces held it closed until the chamber pressure had dropped to a safe level. The rifle was tested by the British Government in 1932 and it was described as being the most promising arm of its type that the Small Arms Committee had then seen. In spite of a magazine capacity of only ten rounds it was reported to have fired 140 rounds in three minutes, a remarkable performance. Unfortunately however the breech, although safe, began to open when the chamber pressure was still quite high. This led to difficulties of extraction and in order to overcome this Pedersen had his cartridges dry waxed. This, reasonably enough, was not acceptable in a military cartridge which would have to be stored world-wide in a variety of conditions and climates, so the Pedersen was not finally accepted after all. This was a pity because it was a neat, handy weapon which shot well and its cartridge was of exceptionally good performance. It is possible that it might have performed well with a fluted breech, which was later designed for this type of contingency, but by that time better self-loading rifles were available. It could fairly be argued that this weapon should be listed under the United States. As however the model illustrated was made in England for test by the British Government for possible use by the British Army it seems reasonable to include it under British weapons.

Great Britain

Great Britain
NUMBER 4 AND NUMBER 5 RIFLES

Great Britain
L1A1 RIFLE

A modified FN, the L1 is currently the standard rifle of the British Army, although it may be replaced in the 1980s by the 4·85mm Individual Weapon. Note the Trilux night sight.

NUMBER 4 AND NUMBER 5 RIFLES		L1A1 RIFLE	
Length:	44·5" (1130mm)	**Length:**	44·5" (1130mm)
Weight:	9·1lb (4·12kg)	**Weight:**	9·5lb (4·31kg)
Barrel:	25·2" (640mm)	**Barrel:**	31" (533mm)
Calibre:	·303"	**Calibre:**	7·62mm
Rifling:	5 groove l/hand	**Rifling:**	4 groove r/hand
Operation:	Bolt	**Operation:**	Gas
Feed:	10-round box	**Feed:**	20-round box
Muz Vel:	2440 f/s (743 m/s)	**Muz Vel:**	2800 f/s (854 m/s)
Sights:	1300 yds (1189m)	**Sights:**	600 yds (549m)

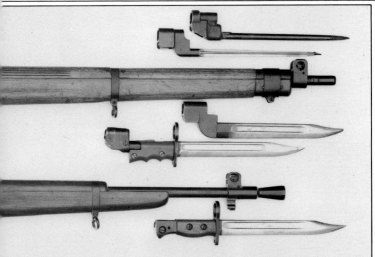

Upper: Seen here with its bayonets, the British Number 4 rifle was mainly produced in Canada and the USA from 1941 onward.

Lower: The shorter Number 5 rifle, designed for jungle fighting.

·303" SAA Ball
·303" SAA Ball
7·62mm NATO
·303" SAA Ball

NUMBER 4 AND
NUMBER 5 RIFLES

By 1928 the British Government had developed a new service rifle, similar in general appearance and capacity to the Lee-Enfield but a good deal easier to mass-produce. This new rifle, the Number 4, was a most serviceable arm, its main difference from its predecessor being its aperture sight. It was produced from 1941 onwards, mainly in Canada and the United States, although some were made in England. It underwent some modifications, mainly in the substitution of a simple two-range flip back sight for the earlier and more complex one, and some were made with two-groove rifling, but otherwise remained substantially unchanged, the main feature being perhaps the variety of bayonets made to fit it. Selected specimens were fitted with No 32 telescopic sights and detachable cheek-rests and were successfully used as sniper rifles. It remained in service in the British regular army until 1957,

and some are still used by cadets. It was popular as a target rifle and the current British sniper rifle is based on it. Experience in the Far East showed the need for a shorter weapon for jungle fighting and by 1944 a new Number 5 rifle had been developed. It was closely based on the Number 4 but was five inches shorter and 1·6lb lighter. Its shorter barrel made a flash hider necessary and reduced its muzzle velocity slightly. It was sighted to 800 yards and fitted with a recoil pad to counteract the extra recoil resulting from its reduced weight.

Above: *With a Number 4 rifle slung, General Orde Wingate, creator of the Chindit jungle fighters in Burma during World War II, boards a Dakota (C-47) aircraft. The shorter Number 5 rifle was developed at this time for use in the Far East.*

Above left: *A sniper from a New Zealand unit, armed with a Number 4 rifle, takes up his position in the ruins of Cassino during the Italian campaign of 1944.*

Top: *A rifleman of the 1st Nyasaland Battalion, King's African Rifles, uniformed for jungle warfare—complete with rope for crossing swollen streams—and armed with a Number 5 rifle, in 1952.*

Great Britain
L1A1 RIFLE

Once the EM 2 rifle had been rejected, the British Army decided to adopt a new self-loading rifle firing the standard NATO cartridge. After extensive tests it was decided to adopt the Belgian FN rifle, which was already in use by many other contries and this, with a number of modifications, became the L1A1. The British version is a self-loader only and will not fire bursts; nor did the British Army adopt the heavy barrelled version which some countries use as their squad or section light machine gun.

The early rifle has been modified in some respects, particularly as regards the use of glass fibre instead of wood, but still remains unchanged in principle. It is gas-operated, and capable of thirty or forty well-aimed shots a minute and is generally a sound and reliable weapon. Its principal disadvantage is its length; when

it was adopted the British had commitments world-wide and needed a rifle for all purposes but now that her role is largely confined to North-West Europe, she is likely to change to a shorter assault rifle, which would be a good deal more manageable when operating from armoured fighting vehicles and would also be capable of automatic fire in street fighting or other close-quarter work. The specimen

llustrated is fitted with a night sight. There are a variety of these, varying from the simple foresight with a self-powered light source to the Trilux sight shown, which can be quickly and easily mounted. It is self-energizing and easily adjusted for intensity and is useful not only for night work but against indistinct targets by day. It has been in service since 1974, its official designation being the Sight Unit Infantry Trilux.

Above left: *Armed with a British 7·62mm L1A1 self-loading rifle, and hung around with ammunition bandoliers, a soldier of the Royal Australian Regiment/ New Zealand ANZAC forces patrols in the jungle of eastern Phuoc Tuy Province, Vietnam, during the later 1960s.*

Above: *British paratroopers of the 1st Parachute Logistics Regiment. The sergeant holds an L1A1 rifle, the self-loading arm of Belgian origin which has been in service with the British Army since 1974.*

Great Britain

SNIPER RIFLE L4A1

Length:	42.15" (1071mm)
Weight:	9.75lb (4.42kg)
Barrel:	27.5" (699mm)
Calibre:	7.62mm
Rifling:	4 groove r/hand
Operation:	Bolt
Feed:	10-round box
Muz Vel:	2750 f/s (838 m/s)
Sights:	Telescopic

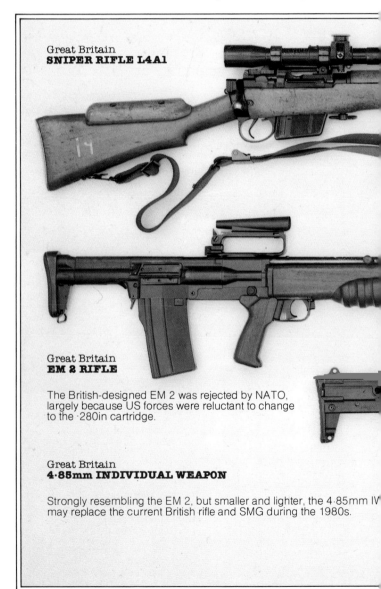

Great Britain
SNIPER RIFLE L4A1

Great Britain
EM 2 RIFLE

The British-designed EM 2 was rejected by NATO, largely because US forces were reluctant to change to the ·280in cartridge.

Great Britain
4·85mm INDIVIDUAL WEAPON

Strongly resembling the EM 2, but smaller and lighter, the 4·85mm IW may replace the current British rifle and SMG during the 1980s.

EM 2 RIFLE

Length:	35" (889mm)
Weight:	7·55lb (3·42kg)
Barrel:	24·5" (623mm)
Calibre:	·280"
Rifling:	4 groove r/hand
Feed:	20-round box
Muz Vel:	2530 f/s (772 m/s)
C. Rate:	450 rpm
Sights:	600 yds (549m) or opt.

4·85mm INDIVIDUAL WEAPON

Length:	30·3" (770mm)
Weight:	8·5lb (3·86kg)
Barrel:	20·4" (518mm)
Calibre:	4·85mm
Rifling:	4 groove r/hand
Operation:	Gas
Feed:	20-round box
Muz Vel:	2952 f/s (900 m/s)
Sights:	Optical

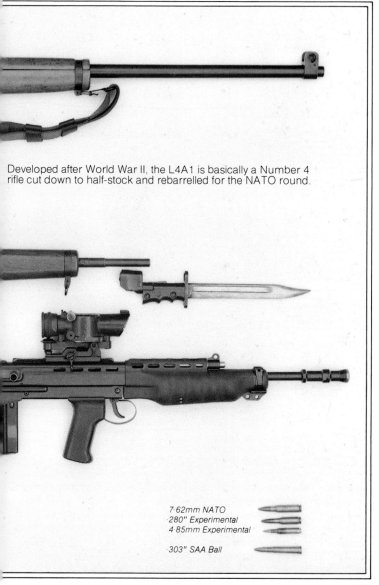

Developed after World War II, the L4A1 is basically a Number 4 rifle cut down to half-stock and rebarrelled for the NATO round.

7·62mm NATO
·280" Experimental
4·85mm Experimental

·303" SAA Ball

Great Britain
SNIPER RIFLE L4A1

Sniping first came into large scale use in World War I and World War II soon proved that there was still a need for it. After 1945 the British Army neglected sniping until their long experience in internal security duties round the world made them think differently. Modern self-loading rifles are not well suited to a telescopic sight, so it therefore became necessary to look back rather than forward for a suitable weapon and it so happened that a commercial conversion of the Number 4 rifle, the Enfield Envoy, was available. It had been developed for target use, principally by being rebarrelled to fire the standard NATO rifle cartridge and by cutting it down to half stock. The Royal Small Arms Factory at Enfield then converted a number of specially selected Number 4s in similar fashion and fitted them with sights which are a modified version of the original No 32 telescopic sight.

Great Britain
EM 2 RIFLE

Soon after the end of World War II work began at the Royal Small Arms Factory, Enfield, on a new assault rifle to replace the existing bolt action Number 4, one of its principal designers being Mr Stefan Janson. The new arm was of somewhat unconventional design with the working parts and magazine housed behind the trigger in a rearward extension of the body, which also had the buttplate attached to it. As the buttplate was in line with the axis of the barrel it was necessary to elevate the line of sight and this was done by incorporating an

optical sight as part of the carrying handle. Although the sight was non-magnifying it did away with the need to focus and align front and rear sights and target. All that was necessary was to align the pointer on the target image which made it very quick to handle. It did very well on trials, its only minor disadvantage being that owing to the situation of the ejection opening on the right side above the magazine the rifle could not be fired from the left shoulder. In spite of its effectiveness NATO, and in particular the United States

Above: *The light and compact 4·85mm Individual Weapon, with a x4 SUSAT sight, is being considered as a replacement for both the L1 rifle and L2 sub-machine gun in British Army service during the 1980s.*

Left: *A British sniper in full camouflage gear presents his 7·62mm Sniper Rifle L4A1 for inspection. This is basically a Number 4 rifle re-barrelled to fire the standard NATO cartridge and fitted with a modified version of the Number 32 telescopic sight.*

who then comprised the backbone of the organization, rejected it, mainly because of understandable American reluctance to change calibre at a time when they had huge stocks of the current cartridge and the almost unlimited capacity to produce more. A few EM 2s were rebarrelled experimentally to take the existing round, but the rifle really needed a major re-design to do this and as time was pressing Great Britain reluctantly abandoned it in favour of a Belgian type of self-loader.

After NATO's rejection of the EM 2 Britain relied for many years on her self-loading rifle. By the early 1970s however it was finally clear than an assault rifle was necessary, partly for reasons of morale but also because the existing rifle was too long and bulky for modern armoured warfare. The weapon finally developed bears a strong outward resemblance to the EM 2 but is small and lighter and mechanically more advanced. It works by the normal method of gas and piston with a rotating bolt, and extensive trials have proved it to be highly effective. It has an optical sight and will fire either single rounds or bursts as required. Its magazine holds twenty of its new rounds which are just under half the weight of the current NATO cartridge, and it can be adopted to fire grenades. There is also a heavy-barrelled version of it which is identical in operation. This has a light tripod and about 80% of the components are common to both weapons. A thirty-round magazine is available for this type, although each will take both kinds of magazine. The gun fires from a closed bolt, i.e. the round is pre-positioned in the chamber ready to fire. This can in theory lead to premature discharge, when the chamber is very hot. so the weapon has now been successfully modified to fire bursts from an open bolt. NATO trials with this and other weapons are still in progress. As the main object of these is to produce a standard cartridge, it would be possible to convert the new rifle to some other calibre if the 4·85mm round is unacceptable.

CEI-RIGOTTI
AUTOMATIC RIFLE

Length:	39·4" (1000mm)
Weight:	9·55lb (4·3kg)
Barrel:	19" (483mm)
Calibre:	6·5mm
Rifling:	4 groove r/hand
Feed:	25-round box
Muz Vel:	2400 f/s (730 m/s)
C. Rate:	Up to 900 rpm
Sights:	1531 yds (1400m)

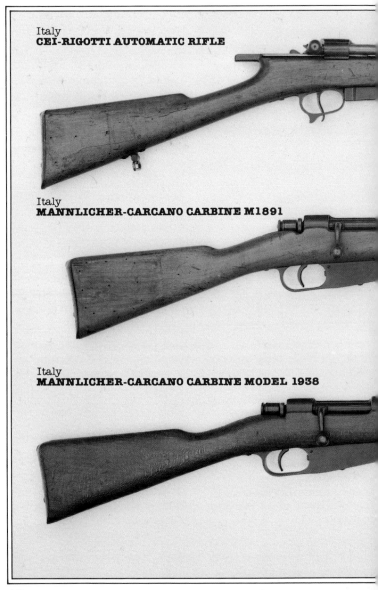

Italy
CEI-RIGOTTI AUTOMATIC RIFLE

Italy
MANNLICHER-CARCANO CARBINE M1891

Italy
MANNLICHER-CARCANO CARBINE MODEL 1938

MANNLICHER-CARCANO CARBINE M1891	
Length:	36·2" (920mm)
Weight:	6·6lb (3kg)
Barrel:	17·1" (444mm)
Calibre:	6·5mm
Rifling:	4 groove r/hand
Operation:	Bolt
Feed:	6-round magazine
Muz Vel:	2300 f/s (701 m/s)
Sights:	1640 yds (1500m)

MANNLICHER-CARCANO CARBINE MODEL 1938	
Length:	40·2" (1022mm)
Weight:	7·6lb (3·45kg)
Barrel:	21" (533mm)
Calibre:	6·5mm
Rifling:	4 groove r/hand
Operation:	Bolt
Feed:	6-round magazine
Muz Vel:	2300 f/s (701 m/s)
Sights:	Fixed 328 yds (300m)

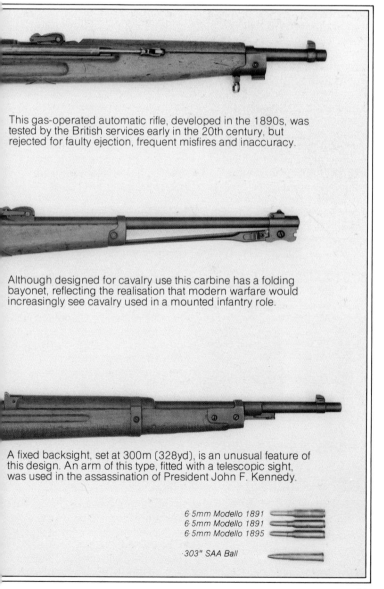

This gas-operated automatic rifle, developed in the 1890s, was tested by the British services early in the 20th century, but rejected for faulty ejection, frequent misfires and inaccuracy.

Although designed for cavalry use this carbine has a folding bayonet, reflecting the realisation that modern warfare would increasingly see cavalry used in a mounted infantry role.

A fixed backsight, set at 300m (328yd), is an unusual feature of this design. An arm of this type, fitted with a telescopic sight, was used in the assassination of President John F. Kennedy.

6·5mm Modello 1891
6·5mm Modello 1891
6·5mm Modello 1895

·303" SAA Ball

Italy
CEI-RIGOTTI
AUTOMATIC RIFLE

Captain Cei-Rigotti, an officer in the Italian Army, appears to have started experiments with gas-operated automatic rifles as early as 1895 when he demonstrated one to his Divisional Commander, the Prince of Naples. Some years were spent in further development thereafter and it was not until 1900 that his efforts were made public in a Roman newspaper, which published a long and laudatory account of his achievements. This included a reference to the use of Mounted Infantry in the war in South Africa, and it was probably this which first drew British attention to the new weapon. Specimens were obtained and a series of tests carried out both by the Small Arms Committee and their Royal Navy counterparts. The rifle worked by a short-stroke piston from the barrel to a rod connected to the bolt, this rod and the cocking handle at its rear end being clearly visible in the photograph, and was designed to fire both single shots and bursts. Although some success was achieved the tests were generally unfavourable, both authorities commenting on the difficulties of ejection and the high rate of misfires, although these may possibly have been due to the fact that the ammunition used had been exposed to seawater on the voyage from Italy. It was also reported that the bolt came so far to the rear in operation that accurate fire was impossible, and some adverse comment was made on the general quality of the workmanship, which was perhaps unfair. It is clear, nearly eighty years later, that the rifle had great potential and many of its features have been copied.

Italy
MANNLICHER-CARCANO
CARBINE M1891

The Model 91 weapons were the first of a series developed for the Italian Army towards the end of the 19th Century. In spite of the inclusion of the word Mannlicher in its official title, it was primarily of Mauser design, the only remaining feature of Mannlicher origin being the six-round clip with which the weapons were loaded and which remained in the magazine until the last round had been fired. They were developed at Turin by S. Carcano, a designer at the Italian Government Arsenal there, and the name of General Parravicino, President of the Italian Small Arms Committee, is often associated with them. The first of the series was a full-

Italian artillerymen armed with Mannlicher-Carcano M1891s: China Relief Expedition, 1900.

length infantry rifle, but this was closely followed by the weapon illustrated, the Model 91 cavalry carbine which actually went into service in 1893. In those days of course, the cavalry still rode horses and therefore needed a short, handy weapon which could be carried either slung across their backs or in a scabbard or bucket on the saddle. The cavalry of most nations at that time were still inclined to delude themselves as to the superiority of the sword and professed to regard firearms as of little importance but the pretence was wearing thin. One feature of the Model 91 carbine is its folding bayonet which indicates that even then the Italian cavalry understood that it might have to act as Mounted Infantry and fight on foot. One interesting feature of these early models, which were otherwise undistinguished, was that their rifling was of the type known as progressive twist, i.e. the degree of twist increased progressively towards the muzzle. This was a system originally experimented with by the English inventor, Metford, but soon abandoned as being not worth the increased difficulties of manufacture. The Model 91s were succeeded by a whole series of others, all of similar principle and differing only in detail. These included a model 1938 carbine almost identical with the one illustrated except that it had a fixed backsight. It is illustrated immediately below this entry.

Italy
MANNLICHER-CARCANO CARBINE MODEL 1938

In the course of their Abyssinian campaign of 1936-38 the Italians were somewhat disconcerted to find that their 6·5mm cartridge lacked stopping power. In 1938 therefore they provisionally introduced a 7·35mm round and developed a modified version of their earlier Model 91 to fire it. This new project was however short-lived because when the Italians entered the war in 1940 they were naturally reluctant to embark at the same time on a major change of calibre, so they reverted to their 6·5mm round. There are thus two versions of the Model 1938 carbine, which except for calibre are virtually indistinguishable, the one illustrated being an example of the later reversion to the small calibre. One of its unusual features was the abandonment of the tangent backsight in favour of a fixed one, set at 300 metres. This model 1938 carbine is of considerable interest as being of the type used to assassinate President Kennedy in November, 1963. The particular weapon was an item of Italian war surplus, fitted with a cheap Japanese telescope and purchased by mail order for a few dollars, and it seems to have been an odd choice. The Carcano has no great reputation for accuracy and although its bolt works smoothly enough, the rate of fire must have been slowed down by the telescope. It is notoriously difficult to shoot rapidly through this type of sight, particularly on a carbine with a good deal of recoil, and there has been speculation as to whether the three shots known to have been fired could have come from a single weapon of this type.

MEIJI CARBINE
38th YEAR TYPE

Length:	34·2" (868mm)
Weight:	7·3lb (3·3kg)
Barrel:	19·2" (487mm)
Calibre:	6·5mm
Rifling:	4 groove r/hand
Operation:	Bolt
Feed:	5-round magazine
Muz Vel:	2400 f/s (732 m/s)
Sights:	2188 yds (2000m)

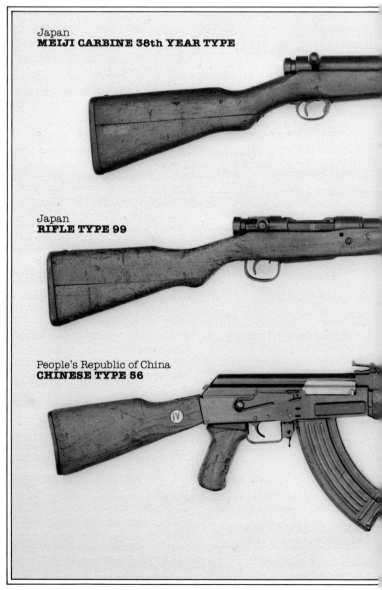

Japan
MEIJI CARBINE 38th YEAR TYPE

Japan
RIFLE TYPE 99

People's Republic of China
CHINESE TYPE 56

RIFLE TYPE 99		**CHINESE TYPE 56**	
Length:	44" (1117mm)	**Length:**	34·65" (880mm)
Weight:	8·6lb (3·90kg)	**Weight:**	9·45lb (4·3kg)
Barrel:	25·75" (655mm)	**Barrel:**	16·34" (415mm)
Calibre:	7·7mm	**Calibre:**	7·62mm intermediate
Rifling:	4 groove r/hand	**Rifling:**	4 groove r/hand
Operation: Bolt		**Feed:**	30-round box
Feed:	5-round box	**Muz Vel:**	2350 f/s (717 m/s)
Muz Vel:	2350 f/s (715 m/s)	**C. Rate:**	600 rpm
Sights:	2625 yds (2400m)	**Sights:**	875 yds (800m)

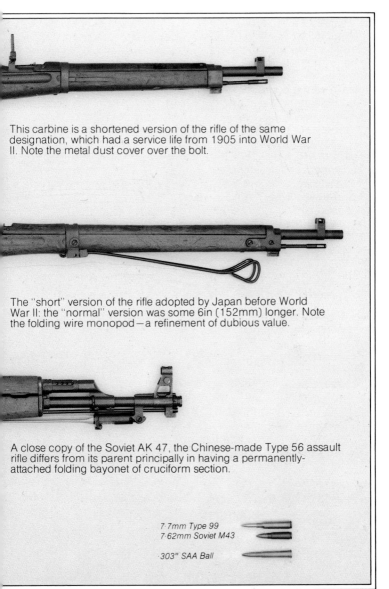

This carbine is a shortened version of the rifle of the same designation, which had a service life from 1905 into World War II. Note the metal dust cover over the bolt.

The "short" version of the rifle adopted by Japan before World War II: the "normal" version was some 6in (152mm) longer. Note the folding wire monopod—a refinement of dubious value.

A close copy of the Soviet AK 47, the Chinese-made Type 56 assault rifle differs from its parent principally in having a permanently-attached folding bayonet of cruciform section.

7·7mm Type 99
7·62mm Soviet M43

·303" SAA Ball

Japan
MEIJI CARBINE
38th YEAR TYPE

Japan made a remarkable change from a medieval to a modern state in the second half of the 19th Century. Her first rifle was a single shot bolt action model of 11mm calibre which appeared in 1887 but which was replaced almost immediately by a rifle of smaller 8mm calibre with a tube magazine. Her war with China in 1894 showed some defects in her armament and a commission headed by Colonel Arisaka was appointed to investigate the whole matter and make recommendations for improvement. The result was a series of Mauser type rifles, first adopted in 1897 and often known as Arisaka rifles. Their alternative title was the Meiji 30th year type, having been made in the 30th year of the rule of Emperor Meiji. Rifles of this type were used in the war against Russia in 1904-5 and a number were purchased by the British in 1914 to train

their new Armies. The 38th year type came into use in 1905 and was an improved version of the earlier model. It had a long life, being used in World War II. The 38th year carbine was simply a shortened version of the rifle for use by arms other than infantry, and would take the standard bayonet. It had a metal dust cover over its bolt, similar to the one on the British Lee-Metford, but it proved very noisy in close-quarter jungle fighting. In many ways it would have been a better service weapon for the infantry than the long rifle, being much handier. Like most carbines however it suffered from fairly heavy recoil. There was a 1944 version with folding bayonet.

Japan
RIFLE TYPE 99

Japanese experience in China in the 1930s (like that of the Italians in the same period) showed the need for a more powerful cartridge than the 6 5mm they then used, and

A US observer of the Russo-Japanese War took this photograph of a Japanese infantryman taking aim with his Meiji 30th Year Type rifle. The 38th Year Type of 1905 was an improved version.

after a good deal of experiment they settled in 1939 for a rifle built to fire a rimless version of their 7·7mm round already used in their 1932 model medium machine gun. The original intention of the Japanese had been to use a carbine, which would have been a good deal handier type of weapon in view of the small size of most of their soldiers. Carbines however, particularly when firing powerful rounds, inevitably have increased recoil, which would adversely affect any lightweight soldiers, however tough and hardy they might be. As a compromise the new rifle, which was designated the Type 99, was made in two lengths, a 'short' rifle in line with modern European custom, and a 'normal' version some six inches longer, the one illustrated being of the shorter type. This new rifle had a rather odd attachment in the shape of a folding wire monopod which was designed to support the rifle when fired from the prone position, but although of some theoretical advantage it can have been of little practical value due to its lack of rigidity. The backsight was also fitted with two graduated horizontal extensions to right and left, intended to be used to give a degree of lead when firing at crossing aircraft; nothing is known regarding their effectiveness. The Type 99 was not widely used in World War II.

People's Republic of China
CHINESE TYPE 56

The Chinese fought their war against the United Nations in Korea with a considerable mixture of outdated weapons mainly of American, Russian, or British origin, but after it was over the Russians started arming their fellow Communists with a variety of more up to date Russian arms notably the SKS carbine, the AK 47 assault rifle, and the RPD light machine gun, all of which fired the same 7·62mm intermediate cartridge. The demand however was enormous and as soon as they were able to do so the Chinese set up their own factories to manufacture military weapons. As there was considerable urgency over the matter, the Chinese wasted no time in trying to produce new or original designs, but simply stuck as closely to the originals as their own somewhat less sophisticated manufacturing techniques allowed them. The weapon which they originally concentrated on was a locally developed version of the SKS, but this now seems to have been relegated to a training role in favour of their Type 56 assault rifle. Mechanically this is a very close copy of the original AK 47, the principal difference being a permanently attached folding bayonet of cruciform section. Although this is a very old idea, the Chinese are by·now the only country still using it, all others having opted for a detachable knife-type bayonet which the soldier can use as a general purpose implement, which is what most modern bayonets are now used for.

Chinese-made Type 56 rifles were extensively used in Vietnam by the Viet Cong who found them to be ideal weapons for soldiers who were mostly small and slight by Western standards; the specimen illustrated is one of the many captured there by the American Army. They are also found in considerable numbers in the Yemen and other Middle East countries and as insurgent weapons in African nations.

MOSIN-NAGANT CARBINE MODEL 1944

Length:	40" (1016mm)
Weight:	8·9lb (4kg)
Barrel:	20·4" (518mm)
Calibre:	7·62mm
Rifling:	4 groove r/hand
Operation:	Bolt
Feed:	5-round magazine
Muz Vel:	2700 f/s (823 m/s)
Sights:	1093 yds (1000m)

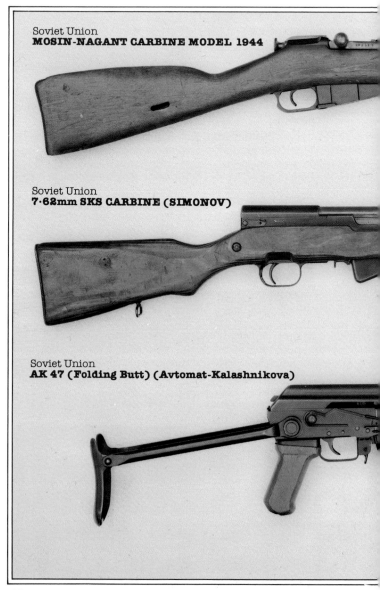

Soviet Union
MOSIN-NAGANT CARBINE MODEL 1944

Soviet Union
7·62mm SKS CARBINE (SIMONOV)

Soviet Union
AK 47 (Folding Butt) (Avtomat-Kalashnikova)

7·62mm SKS CARBINE (SIMONOV)		**AK 47 (Folding Butt) (Avtomat-Kalashnikova)**	
Length:	40·2" (1022mm)	**Length:**	34·65" (880mm)
Weight:	8·5lb (3·86kg)	**Weight:**	9·45lb (4·3kg)
Barrel:	20·5" (521mm)	**Barrel:**	16·34" (415mm)
Calibre:	7·62mm	**Calibre:**	7·62mm
Rifling:	4 groove r/hand	**Rifling:**	4 groove r/hand
Operation:	Gas	**Feed:**	30-round box
Feed:	10-round box	**Muz Vel:**	2350 f/s (717 m/s)
Muz Vel:	2410 f/s (735 m/s)	**C. Rate:**	600 rpm
Sights:	1093 yds (1000m)	**Sights:**	875 yds (800m)

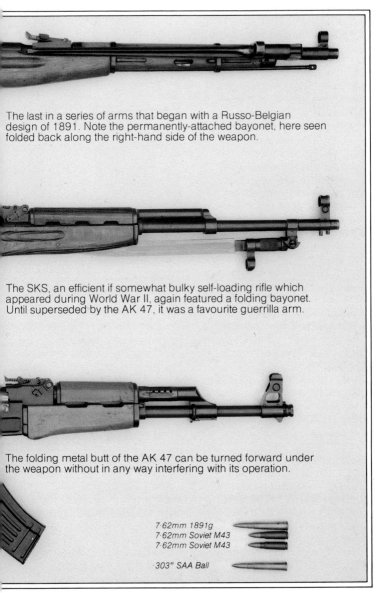

The last in a series of arms that began with a Russo-Belgian design of 1891. Note the permanently-attached bayonet, here seen folded back along the right-hand side of the weapon.

The SKS, an efficient if somewhat bulky self-loading rifle which appeared during World War II, again featured a folding bayonet. Until superseded by the AK 47, it was a favourite guerrilla arm.

The folding metal butt of the AK 47 can be turned forward under the weapon without in any way interfering with its operation.

7·62mm 1891g
7·62mm Soviet M43
7·62mm Soviet M43

·303" SAA Ball

Soviet Union
MOSIN-NAGANT CARBINE MODEL 1944

The first Mosin-Nagant arms were developed by Colonel Sergei Mosin of the Russian Artillery, and a Belgian designer named Nagant. The 1891 model was the first of the modern small-bore bolt-action magazine rifles to be used by Russia and virtually all her later rifles of the type are based on it. The basic rifle was of fairly orthodox design and took a somewhat outmoded socket bayonet. There were several variations, chiefly in the length of the barrel. The calibre was originally measured in an old Russian unit known as a line and equivalent to 1/10″ As a result they were often known as 'three-line' rifles until the metric system was introduced after the Revolution. Their sights were also calibrated in arshins, another ancient measurement based on the human pace. Many of these earlier rifles were made in other European countries, and during World War I the United States manufactured one and a half million of them for Russia. The next major change came in 1930, although even this was little more than a general modernization of the early type. It did however lead to the production of a sniper version with a telescopic sight. The weapon illustrated was introduced towards the end of World War II and was the very last of the Mosin-Nagant series to be made. It was still very similar to its predecessors, but incorporated a permanently attached bayonet which folded back along the right side of the rifle when not in use. It had an unpleasant chisel point which can be seen just behind the backsight in the illustration of the carbine .

Soviet Union
7·62mm SKS CARBINE (SIMONOV)

This was an early type of self-loader, developed and produced by Russia in the course of World War II. It was a gas operated weapon of orthodox appearance, and was designed to fire an 'intermediate' round of the type originally developed by the German Army for their MP 43/44. It had a magazine capacity of ten rounds which could be loaded either separately or by clips, and was equipped with a folding bayonet of bladed type, which turned back under the barrel when not required. The woodwork was of laminated beech, heavily varnished. The SKS

Escorted by a guard with a slung SKS (Simonov) carbine, an East German couple are turned back at the Berlin border, 1961. Soldier in foreground is armed with a slung PPSh 41 sub-machine gun.

was an efficient weapon, if somewhat heavy, and the cartridge gave adequate power at the sort of ranges envisaged in modern war, which by Russian techniques were of the order of three or four hundred metres. This was probably a perfectly practical maximum for an Army well equipped with machine guns of one kind or another. The SKS was used and manufactured by many Communist bloc countries, and a number of non-communist states, among them Egypt, were equipped with it. At one period it became very much a standard guerrilla arm, being widely used in Aden, the Yemen, Oman and elsewhere in the Middle East, but by now it has

been largely superseded by the ubiquitous AK 47 in its various forms, and survives mainly as an arm for watchmen, village home guards, and other relatively humble organizations which do not require advanced firearms.

Soviet Union
AK 47 (Folding Butt) (Avtomat-Kalashnikova)

The earliest versions of the AK 47, which came into use in the Russian Army in 1951, had wooden butts. These, like many other early Soviet arms, were of poor quality timber which detracted greatly from the otherwise excellent quality and finish of the new arms as a whole. Soon afterwards there appeared an alternative version with a folding metal butt which could if required be turned forward under the weapon without affecting its use. This type was probably originally intended for use by airborne troops, but its compactness made it easily concealed and therefore an obvious weapon for guerrillas, terrorists, and similar irregular organizations and it now appears to be almost universally used all over the world in this role. Apart from its compactness the AK 47 has certain other obvious advantages in this respect; it is strongly made and shoots as well as an orthodox rifle to four hundred metres with the additional advantage of automatic fire if needed. Perhaps even more important is its general simplicity; the sort of organizations using it rarely have the time or facilities for extensive training of recruits so that something which can be taught quickly to an individual with no previous experience of firearms is useful.

Soviet Union
AK 47

Finland
M62 ASSAULT RIFLE (THE VALMET)

AK 47

Length:	34·65" (880mm)
Weight:	9·45lb (4·3kg)
Barrel:	16·34" (415mm)
Calibre:	7·62mm intermediate
Rifling:	4 groove r/hand
Feed:	30-round box
Muz Vel:	2350 f/s (717 m/s)
C. Rate:	600 rpm
Sights:	875 yds (800m)

M62 ASSAULT RIFLE (THE VALMET)

Length:	36" (914mm)
Weight:	8lb (3·6kg)
Barrel:	16·5" (419mm)
Calibre:	7·62mm
Rifling:	4 groove r/hand
Feed:	30-round box
Muz Vel:	2350 f/s (718 m/s)
C. Rate:	650 rpm
Sights:	875 yds (800m)

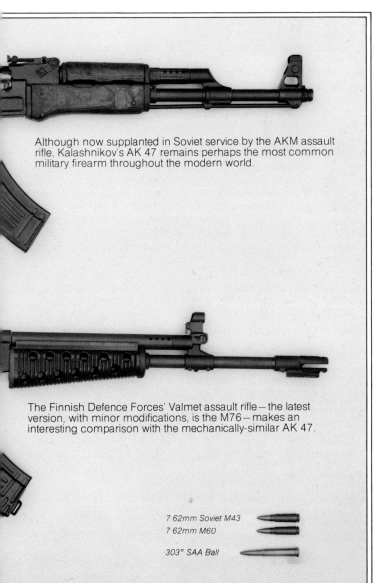

Although now supplanted in Soviet service by the AKM assault rifle, Kalashnikov's AK 47 remains perhaps the most common military firearm throughout the modern world.

The Finnish Defence Forces' Valmet assault rifle — the latest version, with minor modifications, is the M76 — makes an interesting comparison with the mechanically-similar AK 47.

7·62mm Soviet M43
7·62mm M60
·303" SAA Ball

Soviet Union
AK 47

The Russians understood the value of sheer volume of fire, particularly if it could be produced from simple weapons by not very highly trained troops, and in World War II they had armed whole battalions with sub-machine guns. These, however, although effective in their way, suffered from serious limitations in range, but the Russians quickly saw that this disadvantage could be offset by the use of an assault rifle instead. They had seen, and been impressed with, the German MP 44 and as soon as the war was over they set out to produce a similar weapon of their own. In this project they were almost certainly helped by various German designers and engineers who had fallen into their hands. The designer finally responsible for the AK 47 was Michael Kalashnikov and his weapon was officially adopted for use in the Russian Army in 1951. It was in every way an exceptionally fine assault rifle. It worked by gas, tapped off from the barrel and impinging on a piston working in a cylinder above the barrel. This piston took with it the rotating bolt, the whole being thrust forward again by the coiled return spring at the proper time. The AK 47 is accurate and sufficiently heavy to shoot well at automatic up to the sort of ranges likely to be required in modern war, that is, about 300 metres, without undue vibration. It is well made and well finished, being in this respect considerably in advance of most earlier Soviet weapons. It fires an intermediate cartridge which contrary to mistakenly held beliefs is not inter-changeable with the NATO round. The bore is chromed and the weapon is easy to strip and handle. It is designed to take a knife-type bayonet and in later models the wooden butt has been replaced by a folding metal one. The AK 47 has been manufactured extensively by the various Soviet Bloc countries and must have good claim to be considered as just about the most common military firearm in the world today. It is being

Viet Cong guerrillas — an elite band, wearing uniforms like those of North Vietnamese regulars — are armed with Soviet AK 47s.

replaced by an improved version, the AKM, but is still an almost universal arm for subversive and terrorist groups.

Finland
M62 ASSAULT RIFLE (THE VALMET)

Finland has such a long common frontier with the USSR that it is inevitable that she has always been closely connected (by no means always amicably) with her very much larger neighbour. The two countries fought a short but bloody war in 1939-40, provoked largely by Russia's demands for bases which the Finns were not at all prepared to concede, and Finland was eventually beaten though she fought well. Later she joined forces with the Germans in an attempt to regain the parts of the country she had lost but this ambition was not of course realized and after the defeat of Germany in 1945 she was compelled to assent to a peace treaty under which she lost some 12% of her territory to Russia. In view of the long association, Finland has always employed Soviet type weapons,

Finnish soldier armed with M62 assault rifle (Valmet).

locally made in her own factories and often better made and finished than the originals. This reliance on her neighbour stood her in good stead in 1939 when she was able to make use of large quantities of captured arms and ammunition. The first Soviet type assault rifle made by the Finns was developed in the late 1950s and appeared as the Model 1960. Mechanically it was virtually identical to the Russian AK 47 but there were many external differences. The M60, which was made at Valmet, hence its name, had no woodwork on it, everything being made of metal and much of it plastic covered. It had a plastic forehand grip ventilated with a series of holes and a rather ugly tubular butt with a shoulder piece welded onto the end of it. This early model was also unusual, perhaps unique, in that it had no trigger guard in the accepted sense of the term, but only a vertical bar in front of the trigger. The object of this of course was to allow the weapon to be fired by a soldier wearing heavy gloves which are essential in the fierce Finnish winter, but it must have increased the risk of accidental discharge, particularly while operating in forest or scrub. The Model 62, the one illustrated, is essentially similar but of more modern manufacture, making increased use of pressings and riveting. It has the same curved magazine and a tangent backsight mounted on the receiver cover. The three-pronged flash hider incorporates below it a bayonet bar by which the knife-like bayonet can be fixed. It fires the Russian-type intermediate cartridge. Although out of sequence it is included here for comparison with the AK 47.

KRAG-JORGENSEN CARBINE MODEL 1896

Length:	41·5" (1054mm)
Weight:	7·75lb (3·51kg)
Barrel:	22" (559mm)
Calibre:	30/40"
Rifling:	4 groove r/hand
Operation:	Bolt
Feed:	5-round magazine
Muz Vel:	2000 f/s (610 m/s)
Sights:	2000 yds (1829m)

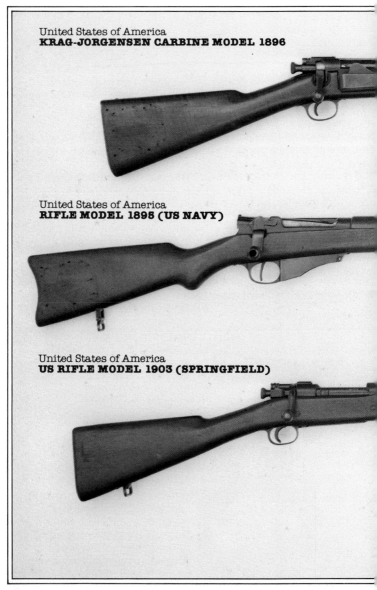

United States of America
KRAG-JORGENSEN CARBINE MODEL 1896

United States of America
RIFLE MODEL 1895 (US NAVY)

United States of America
US RIFLE MODEL 1903 (SPRINGFIELD)

RIFLE MODEL 1895 (US NAVY)	
Length:	47" (1194mm)
Weight:	8lb (3·63kg)
Barrel:	27·25" (692mm)
Calibre:	·236"
Rifling:	5 groove l/hand
Operation:	Straight-pull
Feed:	5-round magazine
Muz Vel:	2400 f/s (732 m/s)
Sights:	2000 yds (1828m)

US RIFLE MODEL 1903 (SPRINGFIELD)	
Length:	43·2" (1097mm)
Weight:	8·7lb (3·94kg)
Barrel:	24" (610mm)
Calibre:	·30"
Rifling:	4 groove r/hand
Operation:	Bolt
Feed:	5-round box
Muz Vel:	2800 f/s (813 m/s)
Sights:	2700 yds (2469m)

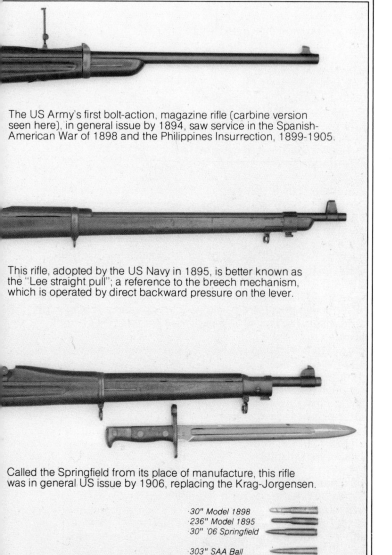

The US Army's first bolt-action, magazine rifle (carbine version seen here), in general issue by 1894, saw service in the Spanish-American War of 1898 and the Philippines Insurrection, 1899-1905.

This rifle, adopted by the US Navy in 1895, is better known as the "Lee straight pull"; a reference to the breech mechanism, which is operated by direct backward pressure on the lever.

Called the Springfield from its place of manufacture, this rifle was in general US issue by 1906, replacing the Krag-Jorgensen.

·30" Model 1898
·236" Model 1895
·30" '06 Springfield

·303" SAA Ball

United States of America
KRAG-JORGENSEN CARBINE MODEL 1896

This was the first bolt-action magazine rifle to be used by the United States Army. It was officially adopted in 1892 to replace the old single-shot Springfield but did not come into general issue until 1894. It was closely based on a weapon invented by Captain Ole Krag of the Danish Army and an engineer named Eric Jorgensen, and the United States paid these inventors one dollar for every one made in America. It was of normal bolt action, its most unusual feature being a five-round box magazine on the right hand side which had to be loaded, one cartridge at a time, through a loading gate which incorporated the magazine spring. The raised thumbpiece by which it was opened is clearly visible in the photograph. There were a number of variations, none of them very important. It was used by the regular Army in Cuba in 1898 although the Militia still had the single-shot Springfield. Soon after the introduction of the Krag-Jorgensen, the United States decided to adopt a new rifle based on the Mauser system and the Krag then disappeared from the military scene. It was an excellent rifle and many converted examples are still in use as sporting rifles in the United States. The specimen illustrated is of interest because it is one of the last carbines used by the United States before the adoption of a standard rifle for general issue regardless of arm or service, which occurred with the introduction of the 1903 Springfield.

The first contingent of the American Expeditionary Force to arrive in England, 1917, parades with Model 1903 (Springfield) rifles and equipment stacked.

United States of America
RIFLE MODEL 1895 (US NAVY)

This rifle is probably better known as the Lee straight-pull which indicates both its inventor and its mechanism. James Lee, a Scot by birth but educated in Canada, eventually became a citizen of the United States where all his experimental work was done. He is probably best known for his box magazine for bolt action rifles; it was widely adopted and his name appears on a long series of British service rifles. Towards the end of the 19th Century he invented a rifle which in 1895 was adopted by the United States Navy who placed an order for ten thousand of them. The rifle was unusual in that it incorporated a 'straight-pull' breech in which direct

Soon after the introduction of the Krag-Jorgensen rifle into the United States Army in 1894 the authorities began to examine the idea of yet another rifle, this time on the Mauser principle, and five thousand infantry models with thirty-inch barrels were ordered in 1901. Before they were made however the United States Army decided that the time had come for a short universal rifle, and had the barrels reduced to twenty-four inches. In this they were probably influenced by their experience in Cuba and also by the lessons of the Anglo-Boer War which caused the British Army to reach a similar conclusion. The new rifle, commonly known as the Springfield after its place of manufacture, had a Mauser type bolt and a five-round magazine with a cut-off, and after some basic modifications, notably the introduction of a lighter, pointed bullet, in place of the earlier round-nosed variety, it was brought into general issue by 1906. It proved to be a very popular rifle, its chief disadvantage, a minor one, being its small magazine capacity, and remained in use for many years. In this time it underwent various modifications, notably one to allow it to be converted to an automatic weapon by the addition of the Pedersen device of 1918 and another which added a pistol grip to the stock in 1929. There was also a target variety, equipped with a Weaver telescopic sight, which was used successfully as a sniping rifle in World War II.

backward pressure on the lever caused the breech to rise slightly, opening as it did so. No manual turning was required, locking worked by an arrangement of cams on the bolt. It was of unusually small calibre and had a magazine capacity of five rounds; it was also the first United States service rifle ever to be loaded by means of a charger. Unfortunately straight pull rifles have no real advantage over the more orthodox turn bolt types, but they do have several disadvantages, chief of which are their complex structure and the fact that their operation, perhaps surprisingly, is more tiring than that of normal types. The United States Navy disliked it very much and it soon disappeared from the service. A sporting version was also made but this also proved unpopular and the model was soon withdrawn, some 18,300 of the 20,000 produced never seeing daylight.

RIFLE ·30 CAL M1 (GARAND)

Length:	43·50" (1103mm)
Weight:	9·50lb (4·37kg)
Barrel:	24" (610mm)
Calibre:	·30"
Rifling:	4 groove r/hand
Operation:	Gas
Feed:	8-round internal box
Muz Vel:	2800 f/s (853 m/s)
Sights:	1200 yds (1097m)

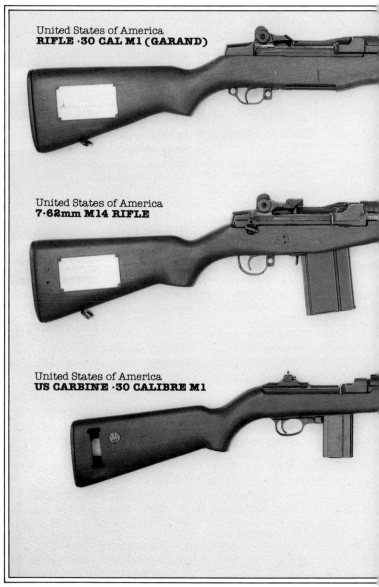

United States of America
RIFLE ·30 CAL M1 (GARAND)

United States of America
7·62mm M14 RIFLE

United States of America
US CARBINE ·30 CALIBRE M1

Length:	44" (1117mm)
Weight:	8·55lb (3·88kg)
Barrel:	22" (558mm)
Calibre:	7·62mm
Rifling:	4 groove r/hand
Feed:	20-round box
Muz Vel:	2800 f/s (853 m/s)
C. Rate:	750 rpm
Sights:	1000 yds (915m)

Length:	35·65" (905mm)
Weight:	5·45lb (2·48kg)
Barrel:	18" (458mm)
Calibre:	·30"
Rifling:	4 groove r/hand
Operation:	Gas
Feed:	15/30-round box
Muz Vel:	1950 f/s (585 m/s)
Sights:	Fixed, 300 yds (275m)

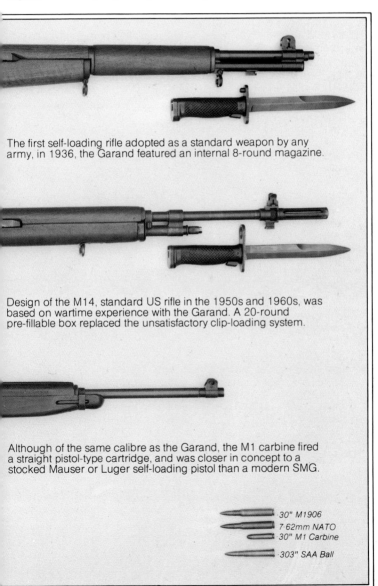

The first self-loading rifle adopted as a standard weapon by any army, in 1936, the Garand featured an internal 8-round magazine.

Design of the M14, standard US rifle in the 1950s and 1960s, was based on wartime experience with the Garand. A 20-round pre-fillable box replaced the unsatisfactory clip-loading system.

Although of the same calibre as the Garand, the M1 carbine fired a straight pistol-type cartridge, and was closer in concept to a stocked Mauser or Luger self-loading pistol than a modern SMG.

·30" M1906
7·62mm NATO
·30" M1 Carbine
·303" SAA Ball

United States of America
RIFLE · 30 CAL M1 (GARAND)

This rifle, commonly known as the Garand, was the first self-loader ever to be adopted by any army as a standard weapon. A whole series of similar rifles were exhaustively tested before it was finally selected in 1936. It was a good weapon, very robust (and therefore heavy) but simple and reliable. It was operated by gas and piston. The magazine had a capacity of eight rounds and had to be loaded by a special charger holding that number of cartridges in two staggered rows of four each. When the last round had been fired the empty clip was automatically ejected and the bolt remained open as an indication to the firer that reloading was necessary. The Garand was the standard rifle of the United States Army in World War II, and was the only self-loader generally used. They were made mainly by the Springfield Armoury and the Winchester Repeating Arms Company, although smaller numbers were also produced by other American arms

companies and after the war a quantity were made by the Italian firm of Beretta. When manufacture finally ceased in the middle 1950s an astonishing total of some five and a half million had been produced. There were inevitably a number of variations to the Garand in its long history, including a National Match model and no less than three sniper rifles, but none of them differed from the prototype.

Below: *US soldiers in training charge with bayonets fixed on their M1 (Garand) rifles.*

Above left: *Fording a stream, a soldier of the US Signal Corps holds his M1 carbine at high port.*

Left: *With his battered M1 carbine slung, a USMC Staff-Sgt fraternises with a young internee in the Pacific, 1944.*

United States of America
7·62mm M14 RIFLE

Before the end of World War II the American Military authorities were working on the concept of a selective fire weapon of assault rifle type. By 1953, NATO having settled on a common cartridge, good progress had been made, and although most European countries opted for Belgian type weapons the United States settled for the M14. This was a logical development of the Garand. Based on war experience a number of important improvements had been made, notably the abolition of the awkward eight-round clip and the substitution of a pre-filled detachable box magazine holding twenty rounds. The new rifle was capable of firing single shots or bursts, and although most were issued permanently set for semi-automatic fire only, a number were fitted with light bipods with a view to being used as squad or section light automatics. They were however only marginally suitable for this role because sustained fire caused them to overheat and there was no provision for changing barrels. A heavy barrelled version was at one time contemplated but never produced, and there was also an excellent sniper version. The M14 saw quite extensive use in the Vietnam war. Some 1,500,000 were made in all, but it is no longer manufactured and although United States NATO forces still use it, it is no longer the standard American rifle. As soon as the NATO countries finally settle on a new cartridge it will become obsolete.

United States of America
US CARBINE ·30 CALIBRE M1

The term carbine, like many military words, has meant different things at different periods. By the end of the 19th Century it was generally used to denote a short version of the standard infantry weapon for use by mounted troops, but in the next few years the universal rifle became common in most armies and the term tended to lapse. Just before World

Above: *The soldier on the wrecked tank holds an M1 rifle.*

Top: *US soldier in white camouflage suit, with M1 rifle, guards Belgian clearing, 1944.*

Right: *A US sniper poses with M1 rifle fitted with telescopic sights and flash eliminator.*

War II the United States Army decided that it needed a new light weapon, intermediate between the pistol and the rifle, as a convenient arm for officers and non-commissioned officers at rifle company level and as a secondary weapon for mortarmen, drivers and similar categories for whom the service rifle would have been awkward. The request, originally made when peacetime financial measures were in force, was at first refused but once war seemed

inevitable it was granted and by the end of 1941 the Army had settled for the M1 carbine and it had gone into large scale production. The M1 was a short, light, self-loading rifle, and although its calibre was the same as that of the service rifle it fired a straight pistol-type cartridge, so that there was no question of inter-changeability between the two. The M1 carbine was an odd, indeed an almost unique, weapon to have been produced so late, since in a very real sense it looked back towards the arms of the stocked Luger or Mauser pistol-type, rather than forward to the sub-machine gun, which at the time of the introduction of the new carbine had amply demonstrated that it had an important part to play in modern warfare. At that period the United States sub-machine gun was however still the Thompson, heavy and expensive to produce, and these considerations probably justified the introduction of a new category of arm.

US CARBINE ·30 CALIBRE M1A1

Length:	36·65" (931mm)
Weight:	5·45lb (2·48kg)
Barrel:	18" (458mm)
Calibre:	·30"
Rifling:	4 groove r/hand
Operation:	Gas
Feed:	15/30-round box
Muz Vel:	1950 f/s (595 m/s)
Sights:	Fixed. 300 yds (275m)

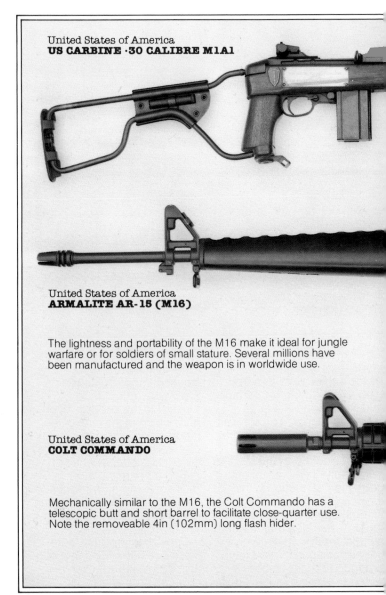

United States of America
US CARBINE ·30 CALIBRE M1A1

United States of America
ARMALITE AR-15 (M16)

The lightness and portability of the M16 make it ideal for jungle warfare or for soldiers of small stature. Several millions have been manufactured and the weapon is in worldwide use.

United States of America
COLT COMMANDO

Mechanically similar to the M16, the Colt Commando has a telescopic butt and short barrel to facilitate close-quarter use. Note the removeable 4in (102mm) long flash hider.

ARMALITE AR-15 (M16)

Length:	39" (991mm)
Weight:	6·35lb (2·88kg)
Barrel:	20" (508mm)
Calibre:	·233" (5·56mm)
Rifling:	4 groove r/hand
Feed:	30-round magazine
C. Rate:	800 rpm
Muz Vel:	3250 f/s (991 m/s)
Sights:	500 yds (458m)

COLT COMMANDO

Length:	28" (711mm)
Weight:	6·55lb (2·97kg)
Barrel:	10" (254mm)
Calibre:	·223" (5·56mm)
Rifling:	4 groove r/hand
Feed:	20/30-round magazine
C. Rate:	750 rpm
Muz Vel:	3000 f/s (915 m/s)
Sights:	500 yds (458m)

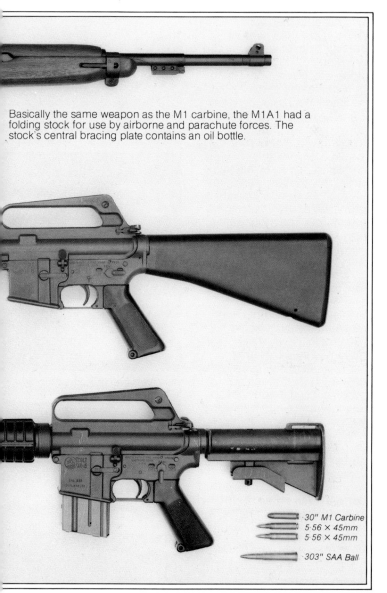

Basically the same weapon as the M1 carbine, the M1A1 had a folding stock for use by airborne and parachute forces. The stock's central bracing plate contains an oil bottle.

·30" M1 Carbine
5·56 × 45mm
5·56 × 45mm
·303" SAA Ball

United States of America
US CARBINE
·30 CALIBRE M1A1

The general details regarding the history and introduction of the ·30 calibre have already been described in the caption for the original weapon of the series. There were however a number of variations, notably the M1A1, which although the same basic weapon as the M1 was equipped with a folding stock, the central bracing plate of which carried an oil bottle. This skeleton stock was pivoted on a pistol grip so that the carbine could be fired if necessary with the stock folded, which made it a convenient weapon for parachute and airborne forces. The true gun enthusiast may feel that this spoils the general lines of the weapon as compared with its prototype and this is to some extent true. The modification however was made at a time when practical considerations were important. The M1 carbine in its various forms was the commonest weapon produced by the United States, the total production reaching the astonishing figure of just over seven million. They were light, handy weapons which in spite of some lack of stopping power fulfilled an obvious need. At one stage a selective fire version was produced which in effect converted the carbine into a sub-machine gun and there was also a version designed to take various types of night sight, no conventional sights being fitted. The two versions were known respectively as the M2 and M3.

US paratroopers round up Germans captured during Rhine Crossing operation, 1945. Trooper on extreme right has M1A1 carbine.

Below: *US Marine fires M16 at snipers in Hue, Vietnam, 1968.*

Centre: *Training with M16s; note blank-firing adaptors.*

United States of America
ARMALITE AR-15 (M16)

The prototype for this weapon was the AR-10 which first went into production in 1955. It was a very advanced arm employing plastic and aluminium wherever possible but it proved too light to fire the powerful NATO 7·62mm cartridge for which it was designed and manufacture ceased in 1962. It was soon followed by the small calibre high velocity AR-15, designed· by Eugene Stoner and made under licence by the Colt company from July, 1959 onwards. This new weapon soon became popular. It was a good jungle rifle and being light and easy to handle by small men it soon found favour in various countries in the Far East. It was quickly adopted by the United States after their intervention in Vietnam and, as the M16, is now their standard rifle (except in NATO). It has no piston, the gases simply passing through a tube and striking directly onto the bolt, which is efficient but means that the weapon needs careful and regular cleaning. It was used by the British Army in small numbers in Borneo.

United States of America
COLT COMMANDO

The Colt Commando is essentially a handier version of the AR-15 and was developed for use in Vietnam. Mechanically it is identical with the AR-15, but with a ten-inch barrel instead of the twenty-inch one of the rifle. This reduced the muzzle velocity slightly and had a rather serious effect on accuracy at longer ranges; it also caused a very considerable muzzle flash which made it necessary to incorporate a four-inch flash hider which can be unscrewed if necessary. The Colt Commando has a telescopic butt which can be pulled out when it is required to fire from the shoulder, and in spite of the limitations of accuracy imposed by the shorter barrel it proved useful in Vietnam where it was used by the United States Special Forces. It is also believed to be in limited use by the British Special Air Service. The reduced accuracy of the weapon puts it into the sub-machine gun class, but in view of its similarity to the AR-15, plus the fact that it fires the same cartridge, it has been left in the rifle section.

The Sub-Machine Gun

A British soldier fires his 9mm L2A3 Sterling sub-machine gun; the standard British weapon of this type since 1953.

The sub-machine gun (SMG) is an automatic weapon which fires pistol cartridges and is light enough to be used two-handed from the shoulder or hip without other support. Such arms were first used to meet an urgent need for close-range firepower in World War I. Italy introduced the Villar-Perosa, a double-barrelled arm firing a 9mm rimless self-loading pistol cartridge, in 1915, but although of obvious utility in trench warfare, it was not as widely adopted as might have been expected.

Next in the field were the Germans, who armed some infantry with stocked self-loading pistols of Luger and Mauser type. These were not true automatic weapons, for the trigger had to be pressed for each shot, but they proved efficient. To avoid too

frequent reloading, magazines with a capacity of 30-plus rounds were produced, and from this it was but a short step to the development of a true SMG (which the Germans designate a machine-pistol).

The MP 18 Bergmann

Hugo Schmeisser produced the MP 18.1, usually known as the Bergmann, in time for use in the German offensive of spring 1918, and some 35,000 were made by the summer of that year. Although Germany's defeat obscured the Bergmann's true significance it was, in fact, the prototype for almost all similar weapons thereafter. Thus, a brief description of its operation will serve for all weapons of the type.

The Bergmann had a barrel just under 8in (203mm) long and a heavy, cylindrical bolt with a permanently-attached cocking handle. Its 9mm cartridges were carried in a "snail drum" magazine (see page 98). To fire, the bolt was drawn back

Soldiers of the Red Army parade with shouldered PPD 40 sub-machine guns. This arm replaced the similar PPD 34/38 during World War II.

manually against a spring and was held to the rear by a sear. When the trigger was pressed, the sear was freed and the spring drove forward the bolt, stripping a cartridge from the magazine, forcing it into the chamber, and firing it. No locking device was needed: the heavy bolt was still travelling forward as it fired the cartridge, and by the time the rearward thrust of the cartridge halted and reversed this movement, pressure had dropped to a safe level. The cycle repeated as long as there was pressure on the trigger and rounds in the magazine. Cyclic rate of fire was about 400 rpm; there was no provision for single shots. The original sighting, to 1000m (1094yds), was unrealistic: the bullet was probably fairly accurate up to c200m (220yds) but, being fired from a low-powered pistol cartridge, had relatively little stopping power at that range.

American Developments

The Allies' only real attempt to produce a similar weapon was the American Pedersen Device, a small machine-pistol which fitted into the breech of a standard Springfield rifle and fired a magazine of pistol ammunition. It was never used in action.

A much better arm was the SMG developed by Colonel (later Brigadier-General) J.T. Thompson, USA; but the first gun to bear his name did not appear until 1921. The Thompson, popularly associated with gangsters and terrorists, perhaps only became "respectable" on its adoption by the US Army in 1938. With the coming of World War II, hundreds of thousands of Thompsons were made for use by the Allies.

None of the other American SMGs of World War II—including the complex Reising and the functional M3 "grease gun"—achieved the fame of the "tommy-gun". It is notable that all American SMGs fired the standard ·45in cartridge for the 1911 Colt self-loading pistol: although an excellent cartridge, this was in many ways too powerful, and made the weapons a good deal heavier to handle than was desirable.

Above: *British troops armed with 9mm Sten Mark 2 sub-machine guns fight through the battered streets of Arnhem in 1945.*

Right: *An American soldier in Vietnam examines a Chinese-manufactured copy of the Soviet 7·62mm PPSh 41 sub-machine gun. The Chinese designated this arm the Type 50 and mass-produced it from 1949-1950 onwards.*

Britain's Wartime Need

The period between the two World Wars saw a steady increase in the use of the sub-machine gun, particularly during the Spanish Civil War. In spite of such clear indications, however, Great Britain took no really positive steps to develop a weapon of this type. This was partly for reasons of economy, but largely because of the country's continuing dedication to the high velocity cartridge; a relic, perhaps, of the devastation wrought by Britain's almost legendary riflemen of 1914. Various models were, in fact, tested; but when war actually broke out in 1939, Britain was compelled to order a large number of Thompsons. They were reliable enough, but heavy and old-fashioned compared with those of the Axis powers, and Britain hastily began to design and produce indigenous sub-machine guns.

The first to go into production was a copy of the German MP 28, which was itself a close development of the original Bergmann MP 18.1. This new weapon, which was known as the Lanchester after its British designer, was issued almost entirely to the Royal Navy, who retained it for many years after the war but

probably used it very little. Meanwhile, the search continued for a light, simple, easily manufactured weapon for mass-production—and early in 1941 there appeared the Sten gun. It was jokingly known to British soldiers as the "tin tommy-gun", and was produced by the million for the use of the British Army and certain allies, and for dropping to partisans in enemy-occupied territories. It went through a series of Marks, becoming more and more simplified for ease of manufacture, and even ran to a silenced version for use mainly by special forces. Even German ingenuity could not improve on the Sten as a simple arm for mass-production: it was copied by Germany, mainly for use by the home defence force, the hastily organized militia known as the *Volkssturm*.

German and Soviet Developments

After 1918, the small remaining German Army had been very tightly restricted in the use of automatic weapons by the Treaty of Versailles. The Bergmann disappeared as a military weapon, although the police were permitted to retain a few for internal security duties. Ways around the irritatingly restrictive treaty were soon found, however, and by 1922 Germany was again making sub-machine guns—the Steyr-Solothurn—in Switzerland under cover of a Swiss subsidiary company. Within a very few years Germany finally abandoned all serious pretence at compliance with the Treaty of Versailles, and began extensive rearmament. In 1938 the German Army adopted the MP 38, commonly known

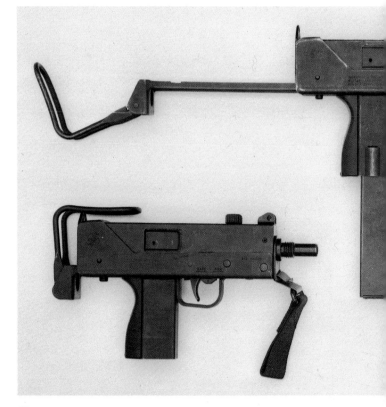

as the Schmeisser, a modern, all-metal weapon with a folding stock. Although this arm underwent a number of modifications during the war, it remained substantially unchanged.

The Russians do not appear to have developed or used a successful sub-machine gun until 1934. During the fighting between the Bolsheviks and the White Russians in 1919, a light automatic weapon was, in fact, used — but it was more of an early type of assault rifle than a sub-machine gun. There was also an early invention by Tokarev, perhaps better known for his revolver; this was a failure, largely because it fired rimmed revolver cartridges which caused constant jams in the magazine. The first forerunner of a long series was the PPD of 1934. This was a sound and reliable weapon, with a 71-round drum which made it rather heavy. Like all later Soviet arms of this type it fired the bottle-shaped 7·62mm pistol cartridge.

The Russians were without doubt the major users of the sub-machine gun in World War II. In the course of their early extensive reverses at the hands of the Germans, a great deal of their industrial capacity was lost or destroyed. The sub-machine gun was easier to make than more sophisticated weapons, and so it was produced by the million. It proved a successful arm in the desperate close-quarter fighting in the various besieged Soviet cities, and whole regiments were eventually armed with it.

Compact and easily carried concealed, the Ingram Model 10 (upper, with silencer) and Model 11 are widely used by security forces.

The Decline of the SMG

Post-World War II development of the sub-machine gun was to be complicated, and largely inhibited, by the rise in importance of a new type of weapon — the assault rifle. This has been dealt with in the introductory essay on the rifle; all that needs to be said here is that it was in essence a sub-machine gun, but one firing a cartridge more akin to that of an orthodox rifle than the pistol cartridge previously used. Naturally, this new arm had its effect on the sub-machine gun, because it could do all that a sub-machine gun could do, and a good deal more besides.

The only new sub-machine gun of any real significance to emerge out of either the USSR or the USA was the American Ingram, which is very much more a weapon for police and other security forces than a military arm. The Colt Commando, it is true, has sub-machine gun characteristics, but it is a lightened version of the Armalite rifle and fires the same ammunition.

Even the nations that did not adopt assault rifles immediately made relatively little progress. Great Britain, having rejected the very advanced EM 2 rifle, finally abandoned the Sten gun and

Above: *US troops in Brest, 1944. The soldier to the left is carrying an M1A1 Thompson sub-machine gun.*

Right: *A Finnish soldier with a 9mm Konepistooli m/31 sub-machine gun, generally known as the "Suomi". This durable weapon was manufactured also in Sweden and Switzerland, and was also used by Norwegian forces.*

Far right: *Menaced by South Vietnamese soldiers, a Viet Cong guerrilla surrenders, holding aloft his American-made ·45in M3A1 "grease gun".*

adopted the L2A1, now the L2A3, perhaps better known as the Sterling. Germany, once allowed to re-arm, experimented with several more or less orthodox designs before concentrating on research into a weapon to fire a new type of caseless round. Israel, having gained independence in 1948, had an urgent need for arms to defend herself against her Arab neighbours, and soon developed the excellent UZI. France developed the MAT 49.

The traditional sub-machine gun was a popular weapon in the Far East and was extensively used by the Chinese in Korea and by the Vietnamese in Indo-China, but it has now been largely superseded by assault rifles of Russian type. This, in fact, is the general trend. The sub-machine gun is essentially a weapon of moderate capacity — but cheap and easy to make — its principal limitation being its relatively weak 9mm cartridge. The only significant improvement would appear to lie in using a more powerful round, but it is difficult to see how this can be done without changing its whole character. On balance, it seems likely that the SMG's military significance will dwindle, but that it will remain a useful arm for security forces for the foreseeable future.

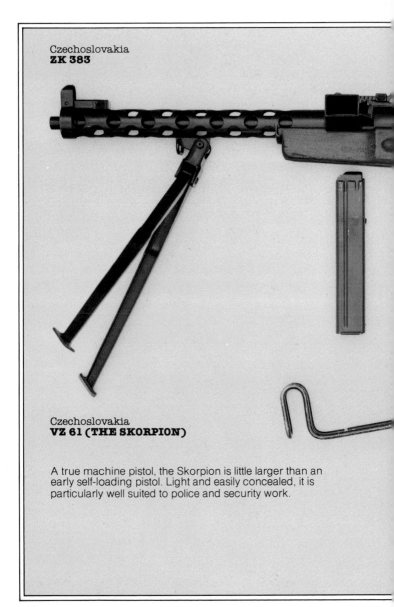

Czechoslovakia
ZK 383

Czechoslovakia
VZ 61 (THE SKORPION)

A true machine pistol, the Skorpion is little larger than an early self-loading pistol. Light and easily concealed, it is particularly well suited to police and security work.

ZK 383		VZ 61 (THE SKORPION)	
Length:	35·4" (899mm)	**Length (f):**	10·65" (271mm)
Weight:	9·37lb (4·25kg)	**Weight:**	2·9lb (1·31kg)
Barrel:	12·8" (325mm)	**Barrel:**	4·5" (114mm)
Calibre:	9mm	**Calibre:**	7·65mm
Rifling:	6 groove r/hand	**Rifling:**	6 groove r/hand
Feed:	30-round box	**Feed:**	10/20-round box
C. Rate:	500 and 700 rpm	**C. Rate:**	700 rpm
Muz Vel:	1250 f/s (365 m/s)	**Muz Vel:**	970 f/s (294 m/s)
Sights:	875 yds (800m)	**Sights:**	Flip, 82-164 yds

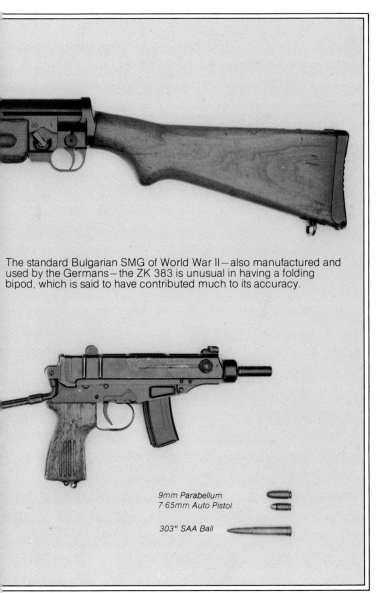

The standard Bulgarian SMG of World War II—also manufactured and used by the Germans—the ZK 383 is unusual in having a folding bipod, which is said to have contributed much to its accuracy.

9mm Parabellum
7·65mm Auto Pistol

303" SAA Ball

This weapon, which was designed by the Koucky brothers at Brno, first appeared in 1933 and was still in production three years after the end of World War II. It is a most sophisticated and very well made weapon, manufactured of precision castings of excellent finish, and cannot have been cheap to produce. It is of particular interest in having a dual rate of fire; this is achieved by removing a weight on the bolt, which increases its rate of functioning.

There is also a quick release barrel, although it is not clear whether this was for changing in action or simply to facilitate cleaning. The ZK 383 will fire either single rounds or automatic as required, the change lever above the trigger being pushed back or forward as necessary. The stud behind it is the push-in safety. The pierced barrel casing carried the foresight and a well made tangent backsight. Another unusual feature is its folding bipod, which when not required for use is turned backward into a recess in the woodwork. This bipod is said to make a considerable

Above: *Czechoslovakian VZ 61 (Skorpion) sub-machine gun with its light wire butt folded forward. This does not affect the operation of the weapon.*

Inset: *A soldier fires the Skorpion from the shoulder, with butt extended. Note his forward grip on the magazine.*

improvement in the accuracy of the gun, but even so it is likely that the maximum setting of 800 yards is optimistic. This was the standard sub-machine gun used by the Bulgarian Army during and after World War II. The Germans continued to manufacture it after they had over-run Czechoslovakia and it was used by their SS troops. A modified version was also produced for police use. It had no bipod and no tangent sight. It is believed that there was a variation of the standard gun with a bipod which folded forward. Some models took a bayonet.

VZ 61 (THE SKORPION)

This is a good example of the rather small number of true machine pistols, its general dimensions being comparable to those of the Mauser pistol model 1896. It is therefore of relatively limited use as a military weapon, except possibly for tank crews, motor cyclists and similar categories for whom a compact secondary weapon is more important than performance. Its small calibre also reduces its stopping power although of course the use of automatic fire helps considerably in this respect. There is also a bigger version, made only in limited quantities, which fires a 9mm round and is in consequence a good deal heavier although similar in essence. The Skorpion works on the normal blowback system. Very light automatic weapons often have the disadvantage that their cyclic rate of fire is unacceptably high, but in this weapon the problem is largely overcome by the use of a type of buffer device in the butt. It has a light wire butt for use from the shoulder; this can be folded forward when not required without affecting the working of the weapon. Although the size and capacity of the Skorpion reduces its military efficiency, it is an excellent weapon for police or other forms of internal security work since it is inconspicuous and easily concealed. Its low muzzle velocity also makes it relatively easy to silence, and an effective model is available which is an additional advantage in this sort of role. It has been sold to many African countries.

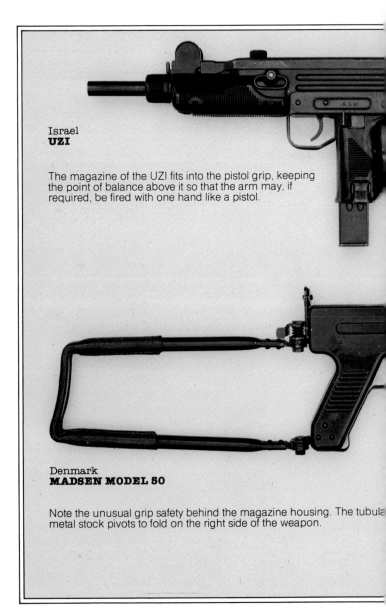

Israel
UZI

The magazine of the UZI fits into the pistol grip, keeping
the point of balance above it so that the arm may, if
required, be fired with one hand like a pistol.

Denmark
MADSEN MODEL 50

Note the unusual grip safety behind the magazine housing. The tubular
metal stock pivots to fold on the right side of the weapon.

UZI

Length:	25·2" (640mm)
Weight:	7·7lb (3·5kg)
Barrel:	10·2" (260mm)
Calibre:	9mm
Rifling:	4 groove r/hand
Feed:	25/32/40-round box
C. Rate:	600 rpm
Muz Vel:	1280 f/s (390 m/s)
Sights:	Flip, 110-219 yds

MADSEN MODEL 50

Length:	31·25" (794mm)
Weight:	6·95lb (3·15kg)
Barrel:	7·8" (199mm)
Calibre:	9mm
Rifling:	4 groove r/hand
Feed:	32-round box
C. Rate:	550 rpm
Muz Vel:	1250 f/s (365 m/s)
Sights:	Fixed

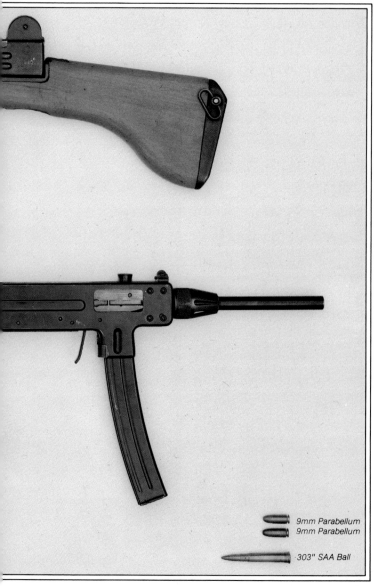

9mm Parabellum
9mm Parabellum
·303" SAA Ball

95

Israel
UZI

At midnight on 14 May, 1948 the British mandate over Palestine ceased, and the Jewish State of Israel was declared. On the very next day the new state was invaded by its Arab neighbours, and there followed nearly eight months of war, at the end of which Israel had not only defended her own territory successfully but had also occupied some of that belonging to her attackers.

In spite of her success however it was clear that she needed a reliable weapon which she could make from her own resources in sufficient numbers to arm the bulk of her population if necessary, and by 1950 Major Uziel Gal of the Israeli Army had designed the weapon illustrated. Production started almost immediately and still continues to date.

The UZI works on the normal blowback principle and is made from heavy pressings in conjunction with certain heat-resistant plastics. The rear end of the barrel extends backward into the body and the front of the bolt is hollowed out so as to wrap round this rear projection. The magazine fits into the pistol grip which affords it firm support and also keeps the point of balance above it, so that the gun can if necessary be fired one-handed like a pistol. It fires single rounds or bursts as required. Most of the early UZIs had a short wooden butt 8 inches long, as illustrated, but a very few were made longer. Later models have a folding metal stock. It is made under licence in Holland and used by many other countries.

An Israeli soldier on the alert with his 9mm UZI sub-machine gun; the design dates from 1950.

The UZI is a most effective arm for street fighting. The model seen here has its folding metal stock fully extended.

Denmark
MADSEN MODEL 50

The first sub-machine gun to be made in Denmark was a type of Finnish Suomi, made under licence by the Danish Madsen Industrial Syndicate in 1940. Production continued throughout the war, the gun being used not only by the Danes themselves but by the Germans and the Finns. The same syndicate has made all Danish sub-machine guns since. The first weapon of the present series was the Model 1946, and the Danes, profiting from wartime advances in mass production, made sure that it was designed in such a way as to be able to take advantage of these improved techniques. The main body, including the pistol grip, is made from two side pieces, hinged together at the rear, so that the weapon can be easily opened for repair, cleaning or inspection. It does, however, have the disadvantage that springs are liable to fall out unless care is taken. The Madsen works on the normal blowback system and will fire single rounds or bursts as required. One of its unusual features is a grip safety behind the magazine housing which (with the magazine itself) acts as a forward hand grip. Unless this safety is in the gun will not function, which makes it impossible to fire it one-handed. The tubular metal stock is on a pivot and folds onto the right side of the weapon. The Model 50, the gun illustrated, is similar to the Model 46, the main difference being the milled knob cocking handle which replaced the flat plate of the earlier model. When the new Model was demonstrated in 1950 many countries showed great interest in it and the delegation from Great Britain was sufficiently impressed to recommend that it should be considered in the search for a new weapon to replace the Sten gun. It was tested against other arms and was recommended for adoption by non-fighting troops if the new British EM 2 rifle made a sub-machine gun unnecessary for the infantry. In the event the new rifle was not adopted and the Sterling was taken into general use. The curved magazine actually belongs to the later model.

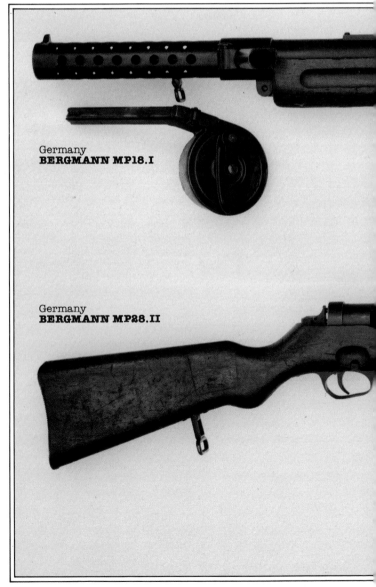

Germany
BERGMANN MP18.I

Germany
BERGMANN MP28.II

BERGMANN MP18.I

Length:	32" (813mm)
Weight:	9·2lb (4·18kg)
Barrel:	7·88" (200mm)
Calibre:	9mm
Rifling:	6 groove r/hand
Feed:	32-round snaildrum
C. Rate:	400 rpm
Muz Vel:	1250 f/s (365 m/s)
Sights:	Flip. 110-219 yds

BERGMANN MP28.II

Length:	32" (812mm)
Weight:	8·8lb (4kg)
Barrel:	7·8" (199mm)
Calibre:	9mm
Rifling:	6 groove r/hand
Feed:	20/30/50-round box
C. Rate:	500 rpm
Muz Vel:	1250 f/s (365 m/s)
Sights:	1094 yds (1000m)

Although it appeared too late to change the course of World War I, this Schmeisser-designed, Bergmann-manufactured arm was, in 1918, the first sub-machine gun to make a significant battle appearance.

Significant changes from the MP18.I (above) include a straight box magazine rather than the complex "snail drum" and ability to fire either bursts or single shots.

9mm Parabellum
9mm Parabellum

·303" SAA Ball

Germany
BERGMANN MP18.1

By the end of 1914 World War I had settled down to a static if bloody business of opposing trenches resembling a two-sided siege on a huge scale and this relatively new type of warfare brought into use a whole host of new weapons; some of these, like mortars and grenades, were simply modernized versions of long obsolete items, but some were genuinely new, and the sub-machine gun comes into this latter category. The first to appear on the actual battlefield was the Italian Villa Perosa of 1915. This was, however, rather complex and in spite of its obvious potential it does not seem to have made any great impression.

The Germans soon began to arm a proportion of their infantry with stocked pistols of the Mauser and Luger type (both of which are dealt with elsewhere in this book), and it was a short step to the introduction of a somewhat heavier version with the capacity to fire bursts. Work on a prototype weapon started in 1916 at the Bergmann factory, the designer being Hugo Schmeisser, the famous son of an almost equally famous father, and by the early months of 1918 it was in limited production. The Germans, always realists, appreciated that at that late stage of the war, when their manufacturing capacity was fully extended, any new weapon would have to be simple to make and the MP 18.I fulfilled that requirement. The techniques of mass production by the use of pressings, spot welding, and pinning were, however, hardly developed so that 'simple' is a relative term when compared with, say, the Sten gun of a quarter of a century later. The Bergmann was machined, and although elaborate milling had necessarily been abandoned, its general finish was relatively good. Its weakest component was its magazine, which was a of a type originally developed for the Luger pistol, and which was too complex and liable to stoppage to be fully reliable. The Germans proposed to have six guns per company; each was to have a number two to carry ammunition, and there were to be three hand carts in addition, which presupposed a type of barrage fire, but it came too late. Its main interest is therefore its influence on future design, which was very significant.

Above: *German soldier advances with his 9mm Bergmann MP28.II sub-machine gun.*

Below left: *German policeman with MP28.II and, apparently, spare magazines of drum type.*

Germany
BERGMANN MP28.II

The MP 18.I issued to the German police for internal security purposes in 1919 had been slightly modified by Schmeisser in the light of practical experience in the previous year. The chief change was a new magazine housing designed to take a straight box magazine of modern type rather than the complex clockwork-operated snail drum which had given a good deal of trouble in the conditions of trench warfare. A few years later the same designer made even more improvements, and as these were sufficient to warrant a new designation the modified MP 18.I appeared in 1928 as the MP 28.II, the II denoting two minor modifications to the prototype. The new gun had some interesting features, chief of which was its ability to fire either bursts or single shots as required. This was controlled by a circular stud above the trigger, which had to be pushed in from the right for automatic, and from the left for single shots. The gun also incorporated an elaborate tangent backsight graduated by hundreds up to a thousand metres, which must have been far outside any practical service range. It was equipped with straight box magazines, but the magazine housing was so designed that it would if necessary accept the old snail drum type. These various improvements did not change its general appearance very materially so that it still resembled the old MP 18. The Bergmann MP 28.II was produced in Germany by the Haenel Weapon Factory at Suhl, but as there were still some restrictions on domestic production of military firearms a great many more were produced under Schmeisser licence by a Belgian company in Herstal, and it was adopted by the Belgian army in small numbers in 1934. The Bergmann soon established a reputation for reliability and was purchased in South America (where it was extensively used in a series of small wars there) and by the Portuguese who used it as a police weapon. Although it was mainly manufactured in 9mm Parabellum, it also appeared in 9mm Bergmann, 7·65mm Parabellum, 7·63mm, and even for the American ·45″ cartridge. It seems probable that its main use was in the Spanish Civil War of 1936-39, where its robust construction made it an ideal weapon for the militias by whom the war was mainly fought. It ceased to be made before World War II, but had a revival in the shape of the British Lanchester.

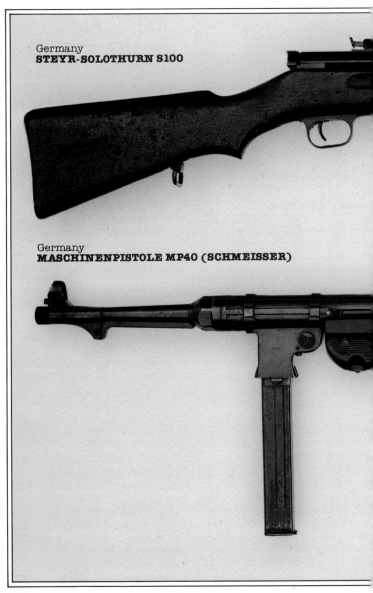

Germany
STEYR-SOLOTHURN S100

Germany
MASCHINENPISTOLE MP40 (SCHMEISSER)

STEYR-SOLOTHURN S100		MASCHINENPISTOLE MP40 (SCHMEISSER)	
Length:	33·5" (850mm)	**Length:**	32·8" (833mm)
Weight:	8·6lb (3·9kg)	**Weight:**	8·87lb (4·024kg)
Barrel:	7·8" (199mm)	**Barrel:**	9·9" (251mm)
Calibre:	9mm	**Calibre:**	9mm
Rifling:	6 groove r/hand	**Rifling:**	6 groove r/hand
Feed:	32-round box	**Feed:**	32-round box
C. Rate:	500 rpm	**C. Rate:**	500 rpm
Muz Vel:	1375 f/s (417 m/s)	**Muz Vel:**	1250 f/s (365 m/s)
Sights:	Tangent. 547 yds	**Sights:**	Flip. 110/219 yds

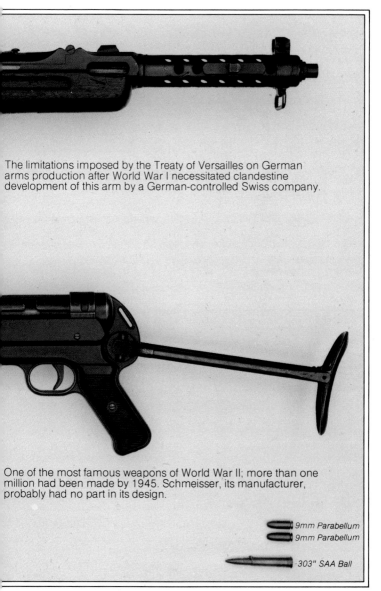

The limitations imposed by the Treaty of Versailles on German arms production after World War I necessitated clandestine development of this arm by a German-controlled Swiss company.

One of the most famous weapons of World War II; more than one million had been made by 1945. Schmeisser, its manufacturer, probably had no part in its design.

9mm Parabellum

9mm Parabellum

·303" SAA Ball

Germany
STEYR-SOLOTHURN S100

By the early 1920s various German designers had resumed work on several new small arms projects, amongst them being Louis Stange of the firm of Rheinmetall which was responsible for the initial development of the Steyr-Solothurn S100. German arms production was of course seriously restricted in the years immediately following World War I and various means were taken to evade the provisions of the Treaty of Versailles. In 1929 Rheinmetall acquired the Swiss firm of Solothurn so as to be able to make and sell arms legally, and it was there that the main developments took place. Once the gun was perfected, however, bulk production was sub-contracted to the Austrian firm of Steyr which started work in 1929. The origins of the weapon are thus to some extent international, but the main initiative undoubtedly came from Germany. The Steyr-Solothurn which was of orthodox mechanism, was extremely well made, the machining, milling and general finish being of an unusually high standard which must have made it expensive to produce. Most weapons have provision for a bayonet and a small number were made with longer barrels. A light tripod mount was also designed but never produced commercially. Most of the production models were also fitted with an unusual device in the shape of a built-in magazine filler. The magazine housing had a slot on top with recesses to take the Mauser pistol type clip, and a magazine locking device underneath. In 1934 two of these guns, one the normal version and one with the longer barrel, were bought and tested by the British Government who were at that time showing some interest in weapons of that type, but although it was well reported on no further action was taken regarding it. Many other countries, however, showed an even greater interest in the gun which was widely sold. At least four South American countries bought it in considerable quantities and it was used in the war fought in the primeval forest of Argentina's Gran Chaco in 1932. It was also adopted by Austria for her army and her police, the gun in this case being modified to fire the more powerful Mauser cartridge, and manufactured in Austria.

Germany
MASCHINENPISTOLE MP40 (SCHMEISSER)

In spite of the success of the Bergmann sub-machine gun in the closing months of World War I the German Army of the 1930s, or at least a powerful faction of it, appears to have regarded the type as being primarily a police weapon, having perhaps had some place in the trenches but none in the new type of warfare for which they were planning. By 1938 however, perhaps because of the lessons of the Spanish Civil War, orders were given to the Erma factory to design and produce a reliable and easily manufactured sub-machine gun, mainly for use by armoured and airborne troops. This was quickly achieved, and in the same year the new weapon had been issued as the MP 38, the first weapon of its type to be adopted by the German Army since 1918. This weapon, with its immediate successors, was to prove one of the most popular and best known sub-machine guns of World War II. It was the first arm of its type ever to be made entirely from metal and plastic, with no woodwork of any kind. Gone was the heavy Bergmann type butt and carefully machined body, and in their place had come a folding tubular metal stock and a receiver of steel tube, slotted to reduce weight. One unusual item was the projection below the barrel near the muzzle; this was said to have been placed there so that the weapon could be fired through the port in an armoured vehicle without the risk that a sudden jolt might cause the gun to be pulled back, still firing, into the vehicle itself. The MP 38, although an excellent weapon, was relatively slow and expensive to produce, and as soon as the early fighting of World War II had shown the desirability of this sort of arm, steps were taken to produce a similar weapon in large quanities. This led to the gun illustrated, the MP 40, which although of similar appearance to its predecessor made more extensive use of pressing, spot-welding, and brazing. Perhaps its most important change was the introduction of a safety device, it having been found (like the Sten) that a moderately severe jolt was sometimes enough to bounce the bolt back and fire a round. A number of the earlier 1938 models were also modified in this way as a result of active service experience. Most of the later MP 40s were made with horizontal ribs on the magazine housing. Only a few, like the one illustrated, were made without them. A later model was fitted with a double side-by-side magazine in a sliding housing. Oddly enough the famous Hugo Schmeisser had no hand in the original design of the MP 38 (although his factory manufactured the MP 40). Nevertheless the name stuck, and the gun became one of the most famous weapons of World War II, some even being used by Allied soldiers in preference to their own sub-machine guns. Over 1,000,000 had been produced by 1945.

Above left: *German soldier with 9mm Steyr-Solothurn S100 SMG.*

Left: *Civil Defence Guards in a South Vietnamese village learn how to use MP 40 (Schmeisser) sub-machine guns, June 1962.*

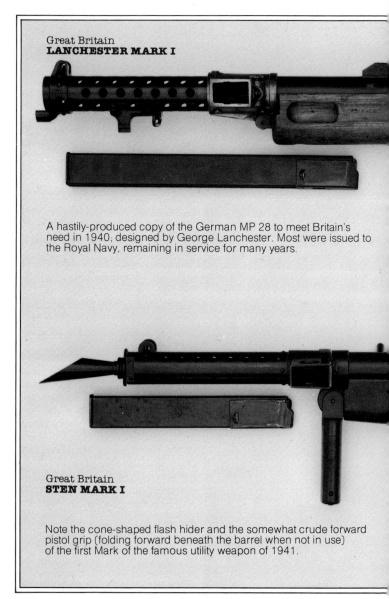

Great Britain
LANCHESTER MARK I

A hastily-produced copy of the German MP 28 to meet Britain's
need in 1940, designed by George Lanchester. Most were issued to
the Royal Navy, remaining in service for many years.

Great Britain
STEN MARK I

Note the cone-shaped flash hider and the somewhat crude forward
pistol grip (folding forward beneath the barrel when not in use)
of the first Mark of the famous utility weapon of 1941.

LANCHESTER MARK I

Length:	33·5″ (851mm)
Weight:	9·65lb (4·38kg)
Barrel:	7·9″ (200mm)
Calibre:	9mm
Rifling:	6 groove r/hand
Feed:	50-round box
C. Rate:	600 rpm
Muz Vel:	1200 f/s (365 m/s)
Sights:	Tangent. 600 yds

STEN MARK I

Length:	35·25″ (896mm)
Weight:	7·21lb (3·27kg)
Barrel:	7·8″ (198mm)
Calibre:	9mm
Rifling:	6 groove r/hand
Feed:	32-round box
C. Rate:	550 rpm
Muz Vel:	1200 f/s (365 m/s)
Sights:	Fixed

9mm Parabellum
9mm SAA Ball

·303″ SAA Ball

Great Britain
LANCHESTER MARK I

In June 1940 Great Britain was in a very serious situation. Her expeditionary force had been compelled to make a hasty evacuation, mainly through Dunkirk, leaving behind it the bulk of its heavy weapons, and there was a very real risk that the victorious German Army would invade the country. One of the weapons which had belatedly impressed the British military authorities was the sub-machine gun, but although large numbers had been ordered from the United States there was no British model available. Arrangements were therefore hastily made to copy the German MP 28 which was known to be reliable, and a British version was designed by Mr George Lanchester of the Sterling Armament Company, after whom the completed weapon was named.

The new weapon was at first intended for the Royal Air Force and the Royal Navy, and in the event most of them went to the latter. The Lanchester, which bore an obvious resemblance to its parent arm, was a robust and reliable gun; British industry had not then been converted to a war footing so that the machining and finish of the weapon was of a very high quality, with a rifle type walnut stock (complete with brass buttplate), and a brass magazine housing. It was also fitted with a standard and boss to allow the ordinary Lee Enfield bayonet to be fixed if necessary.

It had a simple blowback mechanism and could fire either single rounds or automatic as required. It functioned well with most of the standard makes of 9mm rimless cartridge with the exception of the one for the Beretta. There was also a later Mark I which only fired automatic. The Lanchester saw little real service except with the occasional boat or landing party, but it remained in service with the Royal Navy for a long time. Many years after the war most HM ships carried racks of them, chained for security, though rarely used.

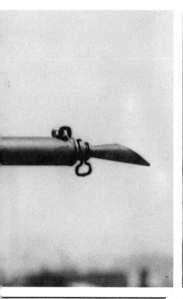

Above: *German PoW escorted by sailor with Lanchester Mark I.*

Above left: *British soldier fires Sten Mark 1 from shoulder.*

Great Britain
STEN MARK I

By mid-1941 large numbers of sub-machine guns were arriving from the United States. Great Britain and the Commonwealth were, however, engaged in raising and equipping new armies and in addition there were urgent demands for supplies and replacements for North and East Africa where British and Colonial troops were operating against the Italians. It was thus clear that there was an urgent requirement for a simple, home-produced sub-machine gun, and by the middle of 1941 a weapon had not only been designed but was in limited production and undergoing user trials. This was the famous Sten, which took its name from the initial letters of the surnames of the two people most closely concerned with its development Major (later Colonel) Shepherd who was a director of the Birmingham Small Arms Company and Mr Turpin, the principal designer, allied to the first two letters of

Enfield, the location of the Royal Small Arms factory where it was first produced. As soon as the few inevitable weaknesses revealed by the trials had been rectified the Sten gun went into large-scale production and in its various forms was to provide an invaluable source of additional automatic fire power to the British forces.

The Sten worked on a simple blow-back system using a heavy bolt with a coiled return spring, but in spite of its simple concept the first models made were still relatively elaborate, with a cone-shaped flash hider and a rather crude forward pistol grip which could be folded up underneath the barrel when not in use. It could fire either single shots or bursts, the change lever being a circular stud above the trigger. It also had some woodwork at the fore-end and as a bracer at the small of the butt.

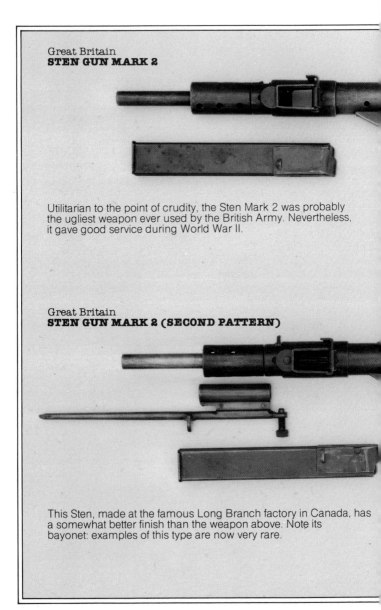

Great Britain
STEN GUN MARK 2

Utilitarian to the point of crudity, the Sten Mark 2 was probably the ugliest weapon ever used by the British Army. Nevertheless, it gave good service during World War II.

Great Britain
STEN GUN MARK 2 (SECOND PATTERN)

This Sten, made at the famous Long Branch factory in Canada, has a somewhat better finish than the weapon above. Note its bayonet: examples of this type are now very rare.

STEN GUN MARK 2

Length:	30″ (762mm)
Weight:	6·65lb (3kg)
Barrel:	7·75″ (197mm)
Calibre:	9mm
Rifling:	6/2 groove r/hand
Feed:	32-round box
C. Rate:	550 rpm
Muz Vel:	1200 f/s (365 m/s)
Sights:	Fixed

STEN GUN MARK 2 (SECOND PATTERN)

Length:	30″ (762mm)
Weight:	6·65lb (3kg)
Barrel:	7·75″ (197mm)
Calibre:	9mm
Rifling:	2 or 5 groove r/hand
Feed:	32-round box
C. Rate:	550 rpm
Muz Vel:	1200 f/s (365 m/s)
Sights:	Fixed

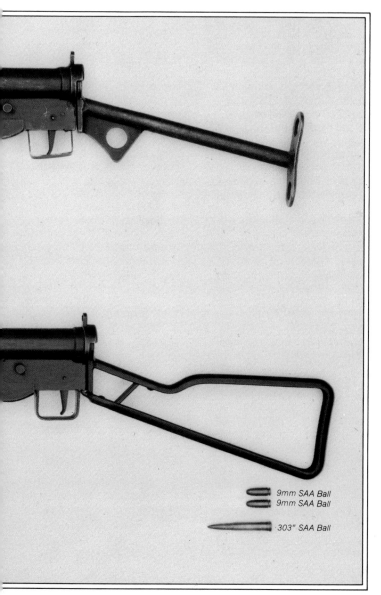

9mm SAA Ball
9mm SAA Ball
·303″ SAA Ball

Great Britain
STEN GUN MARK 2

Towards the end of 1941 a modified version of the Sten Mark I appeared in the form of the Mark 2, this being the first of a long series of changes in the general design of the weapon. The Mark 2 was basically a somewhat stripped-down version of the Mark I, the intention being to simplify manufacturing processes wherever possible. The British gun trade had always prided itself on the finish of its weapons almost as much as on their effectiveness, and the tradition of machined and blued metal allied with polished walnut was a strong one. Nevertheless Great Britain was by this time fighting very literally for her existence and had therefore reached the inevitable conclusion that in emergencies, appearance was not important, only effectiveness, which set a fashion particularly in world sub-machine guns, for many years afterwards. This resulted in the Sten gun Mark 2, the ugliest, nastiest weapon ever used by the British Army. It looked cheap because it was cheap, with its great unfiled blobs of crude welding metal, its general appearance of scrap-iron, and its tendency to fall to pieces if dropped onto a hard surface. Nevertheless it worked, and not only worked but managed to incorporate one or two improvements, notably by attaching the magazine housing to a rotatable sleeve, held by a spring, so that in bad conditions it could be turned upwards through 90° thus acting as a dust cover for the ejection opening. This was a most useful refinement at a time when the British Army

was engaged in large-scale fighting in North Africa. Although the British Army, accustomed to its high quality Short Magazine Lee Enfield rifles and handsomely finished Bren light machine guns, joked about their 'tin Tommy-gun' they got good value out of it. Perhaps one of the most persistent weaknesses in the make-up of the wartime Sten gun was in the relatively poor quality of its magazine, although in the circumstances of hasty construction with poor metal this is not altogether to be wondered at. In particular the lips were very susceptible to damage, which had a serious effect on the feed and led to endless stoppages. It was also found that the dirt and dust inseparable from the fighting in the Western desert, tended to clog the magazine, and although careful attention to cleanliness helped in this respect the problem was never really solved with this particular weapon. Despite these drawbacks, the Mark 2 was an important weapon.

Great Britain
STEN GUN MARK 2 (SECOND PATTERN)

The British and Colonial forces appeared to have an insatiable appetite for Sten guns. Over one hundred thousand of the earlier Marks had been produced by early 1942 and there was still no slackening of the demand. Apart from the inevitable loss and damage in action, more and more troops were being raised and trained, and as the prospect of an invasion of North West Europe, with the probability of extensive street fighting in towns and villages, drew closer the need for sub-machine guns continued to increase.

Apart from the regular armies there was also an increasing demand for light, easily concealed automatic weapons from the various Resistance movements in occupied Europe so that production had to be increased accordingly. There was, however, an equal need for other weapons too, so that no priority could be given. All that could be done was to pare and reduce and simplify so that three weapons could be produced with the same effort and little more than the same *matériel,* that had produced two previously. Much help was given by some of the Dominions, notably Canada, and the weapon illustrated is an example of the type made there at the famous Long Branch factory. Although made to similar specifications to the British version, it is of somewhat better finish, with a more robust skeleton butt. It also has a bayonet, details of which are clearly shown in the illustration, and examples of this are now very rare.

Perhaps appropriately this type was first used in action on the ill-fated Dieppe raid of 19 August, 1942 in which the Canadian Army fought gallantly.

Below left: *Free French soldier in training with Sten Mark 2.*

Below: *British Home Guard men receive instruction from soldier with Sten Mark 2 (Second Pattern), with bayonet fixed.*

Great Britain
STEN GUN MARK 6(S)

The Mark 2 silencer fitted to this arm, which was largely used by special forces, tended to heat rapidly; hence the canvas hand guard fitted over its rear area.

Australia
OWEN MACHINE CARBINE

Designed for use in the jungles of the Far East during World War II, the magazine of the Owen is set vertically above the gun, facilitating the user's movement through thick cover.

STEN GUN MARK 6(S)

Length (s):	35·75" (908mm)
Weight:	9·8lb (4·45kg)
Barrel:	7·80" (198mm)
Calibre:	9mm
Rifling:	6 groove r/hand
Feed:	32-round box
C. Rate:	550 rpm
Muz Vel:	c1000 f/s (305 m/s)
Sights:	Fixed

OWEN MACHINE CARBINE

Length:	32" (813mm)
Weight:	9·35lb (4·24kg)
Barrel:	9·75" (250mm)
Calibre:	9mm
Rifling:	7 groove r/hand
Feed:	32-round box
C. Rate:	700 rpm
Muz Vel:	1375 f/s (420 m/s)
Sights:	Fixed. offset

9mm SAA Ball
9mm Parabellum

·303" SAA Ball

Great Britain
STEN GUN MARK 6(S)

The Mark 2 Sten, which has already been described, probably marked the lowest point in the gun's history, and thereafter quality began to improve. Practically all components were still made in small factories and workshops with no previous connection with the manufacture of firearms, but, perhaps due to experience, the general finish was markedly better than in the early days. There was a Mark 3 (similar in appearance to the Mark 2) which was made in huge numbers and this was followed by a Mark 4, which never went into full scale production. This in turn was followed by probably the best Sten of all, the Mark 5, which was to see service from 1944 until well into the 1950s. Although very similar to its predecessors it was of more

A British Army sergeant fires a Sten Gun Mark 6(S) fitted with an extremely complex sniper scope. This silenced arm was in use as late as 1953.

robust construction with a wooden butt (some with brass buttplates) and pistol grip, and provision was made for it to take the standard bayonet. Experiments had been conducted earlier with a silenced Mark 6 Sten which was sufficiently successful to attract the admiration of Colonel Skorzeny, the famous German who rescued Mussolini, and in 1944 it was decided that a weapon of this type was again required. The standard Mark 2 silencer was thus fitted to the Mark 5, which was then re-designated Mark 6(S). The muzzle velocity of the Mark 5 bullet was in excess of the speed of sound which posed a number of problems in connection with the 'sonic boom' effect, but by drilling gas escape holes in the barrel the velocity was brought down to the required figure. The silencer tended to heat rapidly so a canvas hand guard was laced over it. It was not considered advisable to fire bursts through the silencer except in extreme emergencies. The Mark 6 Sten was used mainly by airborne forces and Resistance fighters in World War II and as late as 1953.

Australia
OWEN MACHINE CARBINE

When Japan entered World War II on the side of the Axis powers, Australia found herself in a precarious position. Most of her small army was engaged in the Middle East and her vast and sparsely inhabited country presented a most attractive target to a warlike race seeking living room. Although there was a well established arms factory in existence at Lithgow, Australia was not then a very industrialized country, but she began to produce arms as a matter of hard necessity. One of her first efforts was an Australian Sten, known, perhaps inevitably, as the Austen, but although by no means a bad weapon it was never popular with the Australian Army.

The first locally designed submachine gun was the work of Lieutenant E. Owen, of the Australian Army, which was adopted in November, 1941 and put into production immediately. It was a well made weapon, if a little on the heavy side, and was an immediate success with the soldiers. It was of fairly orthodox design and its point of balance was immediately above the pistol grip which allowed it to be fired one-handed if necessary. The magazine was vertically above the gun and although this involved offset sights the idea was popular because it helped when moving through thick cover. All Owens were camouflaged after 1943 and provision was made for a bayonet in 1944. The Owen was a thoroughly good weapon and was still in use in the 1960s.

A civilian technician fires the Australian Owen Machine Carbine. Note that, unlike the weapon shown on the colour spread, the metal bodywork between butt and trigger-grip has not been cut away.

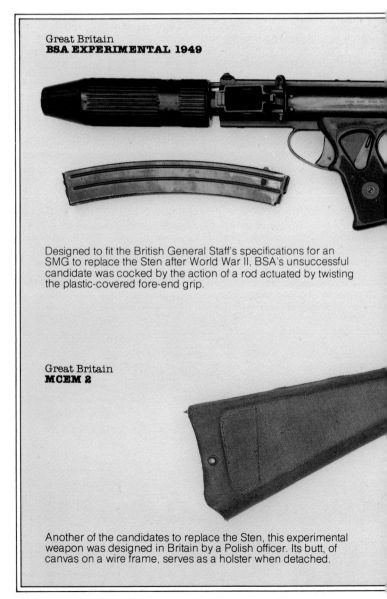

Great Britain
BSA EXPERIMENTAL 1949

Designed to fit the British General Staff's specifications for an SMG to replace the Sten after World War II, BSA's unsuccessful candidate was cocked by the action of a rod actuated by twisting the plastic-covered fore-end grip.

Great Britain
MCEM 2

Another of the candidates to replace the Sten, this experimental weapon was designed in Britain by a Polish officer. Its butt, of canvas on a wire frame, serves as a holster when detached.

BSA EXPERIMENTAL 1949

Length:	27·9" (697mm)
Weight:	6·45lb (2·9kg)
Barrel:	8" (203mm)
Calibre:	9mm
Rifling:	6 groove r/hand
Feed:	32-round box
C. Rate:	600 rpm
Muz Vel:	1200 f/s (365 m/s)
Sights:	100/200 yds

MCEM 2

Length:	23·5" (598mm)
Weight	6lb (2·72kg)
Barrel:	8·5" (216mm)
Calibre:	9mm
Rifling:	6 groove r/hand
Feed:	18-round box
C. Rate:	1000 rpm
Muz Vel:	1200 f/s (365 m/s)
Sights:	Fixed

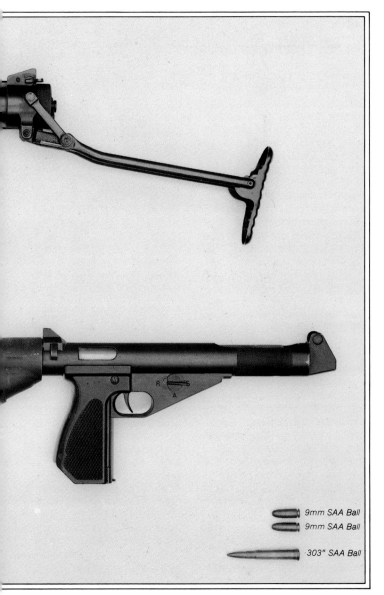

9mm SAA Ball

9mm SAA Ball

·303" SAA Ball

Great Britain
BSA EXPERIMENTAL 1949

The main British sub-machine gun during World War II was the famous Sten, which although hastily designed and roughly finished did its job very well. It was, however, a strictly wartime expedient and even before the war was quite over a new General Staff specification had been issued for a post-war sub-machine gun. This laid down the basic requirements that it should weigh a maximum of six pounds (2.72kg) without magazine, fire at not more than six hundred rounds per minute, have a magazine capacity of between thirty and sixty rounds, and take the No 5 rifle bayonet. Various tests were arranged between 1947 and 1952 for which a number of weapons were entered, among them the Birmingham Small Arms Company's weapon of the type illustrated. It was of conventional blowback mechanism, but was unusual in that it had no cocking handle, that function being performed by a flat rod attached to the plastic covered fore-end grip. When the grip was twisted and pushed forward the rod went with it and the end of it engaged the bolt which was then in the forward position. As the grip was pulled back the rod forced the bolt back also until it was caught by the sear, at which stage it disengaged from the rod. The gun also had another unusual feature in that the magazine housing could be released and swung forward on a hinge without removing the magazine, which was thought to facilitate the clearing of stoppages. It was fitted with a sturdy folding stock which did not interfere with the firing of

Above: *The 9mm Experimental sub-machine gun designed by the Birmingham Small Arms Company and tested, but not accepted, by the British Army in 1949-52, is fired from the shoulder.*

Above right: *The BSA Experimental 1949 SMG is fired from the hip. Curved magazine denotes late model*

the gun when forward, and its change lever was situated above the left-hand pistol grip. Over the years there were a number of variations in the original design; the first model took a straight magazine, later ones being curved as illustrated, and as a result of a change in specification it was modified to take a bayonet. There were also variations in the shape of the forehand grip. The gun was not finally accepted for service and specimens of it are now quite rare.

Great Britain
MCEM 2

Although the Sten gun had served Great Britain well in the period 1941-45 it was not really of the quality required for the post-war army, and after the war was over tests began to find a suitable successor for it. A good deal of design work had been going on, both by native British designers and by a variety of Polish experts, so there was not likely to be any shortage of contenders. The series developed by Enfield were given the collective description of Military Carbine Experimental Models (MCEM), the various types being denoted by a serial number; as a matter of interest the first in the series was the work of Mr H. J. Turpin who had been instrumental in designing the original Sten gun. The weapon illustrated, the MCEM 2, was the work of one of the rival designers, a Polish officer named Lieutenant Podsenkowsky, and it was in many ways an unusual weapon. It was under fifteen inches long and its magazine fitted into the pistol grip; it was also well balanced which meant that it could be fired one-handed like an automatic pistol. The bolt was of advanced design and consisted of a half cylinder 8½ inches (216mm) long with the striker at the rear, so that at the instant of firing almost the whole of the barrel was in fact inside it. There was a slot above the muzzle into which the firer placed his finger to draw the bolt back to cock it, and the gun had a wire-framed canvas holster which could also be used as a butt. It fired at a cyclic rate of one thousand rounds per minute which made it very hard to control and which may have led to its rejection.

Great Britain
STERLING L2A3

Australia
F1 SUB-MACHINE GUN

The butt of the F1 is a prolongation of the barrel. This makes for accurate shooting, but also necessitates an elevated sight line; hence the distinctive metal flap of the backsight.

STERLING L2A3

Length:	28" (800mm)
Weight:	6lb (2·75kg)
Barrel:	7·8" (198mm)
Calibre:	9mm
Rifling:	6 groove r/hand
Feed:	32-round box
C. Rate:	550 rpm
Muz Vel:	1200 f/s (365 m/s)
Sights:	100 and 200 yds

F1 SUB-MACHINE GUN

Length:	28·1" (925mm)
Weight:	7·2lb (3·266kg)
Barrel:	8" (203mm)
Calibre:	9mm
Rifling:	6 groove r/hand
Feed:	34-round box
C. Rate:	600 rpm
Muz Vel:	1200 f/s (365 m/s)
Sights:	Fixed

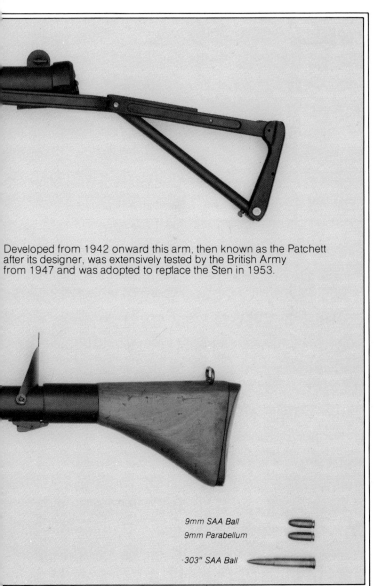

Developed from 1942 onward this arm, then known as the Patchett after its designer, was extensively tested by the British Army from 1947 and was adopted to replace the Sten in 1953.

9mm SAA Ball

9mm Parabellum

·303" SAA Ball

Covered by a comrade with a Sterling L2A3 sub-machine gun, a British paratrooper enters a deserted house, in training.

Great Britain
STERLING L2A3

This gun was designed by a Mr George Patchett and was at first known as the Patchett sub-machine gun. It was originally patented in 1942 and by the end of the war a small number had been made by the Sterling Engineering Company, which had earlier been involved in the production of the Lanchester. A few of these early guns were used by British airborne troops towards the end of the war and their reports on them were encouraging. In the course of the search for a replacement for the Sten this gun was tested against various others in 1947; none was accepted as a result of this first trial because all were considered to need modification. By the time of the next trial in 1951 the Patchett, as it was still then called, was clearly the best gun of those available, and in September 1953 it was finally accepted for

service in the British Army. Its official title was the SMG L2A1, but from the date of its introduction it was commonly known as the Sterling. The gun, which is well made and finished, is of normal blowback mechanism but is unusual in having a ribbed bolt which cuts away dirt and fouling as it accumulates and forces it out of the receiver. This allows the gun to function well under the most adverse conditions. The gun underwent a good many modifications after its initial introduction, notably in the addition of foresight protections, varying shapes of muzzle and butt, and on one light version a spring-loaded bayonet. Some of the earlier models also took a straight magazine. The current version is the L2A3, and the standard Canadian SMG is closely based on it.

Australia
F1 SUB-MACHINE GUN

The standard sub-machine gun of the Australian Forces during World War II was the reliable and well tried Owen gun, which remained in service until 1962. In spite of its excellent reputation the Owen had certain drawbacks, principally its weight, its somewhat high cyclic rate of fire, and the fact that due to the exigencies of wartime manufacture many of its components were not interchangeable which made maintenance difficult. Before the war was over the Australians canvassed the views of many soldiers with battle experience as to what an ideal sub-machine gun should be, so that they had ample information on which to base any specifications for a new weapon. The first gun to be based on these ideas was similar in many ways to the Owen, but much lighter and with its magazine in the pistol grip. This model was not a success and was not developed. However, in 1959 and 1960 two further models were produced; these were known provisionally as the X1 and X2, and after minor modifications became the weapon illustrated, the F1. It was based largely on the original specification and is light in weight and with a much lower cyclic rate than its predecessor. It retains the top magazine of the Owen which was universally popular, although it requires offset sights. The backsight is a shaped metal flap which folds forward over the receiver when not required. The height of this sight is made necessary because the butt is a prolongation of the barrel, which makes for accurate shooting but which requires the sight line to be high. The cocking handle, which is on the left of the body, has a cover attached to it to keep dirt out of the cocking slot. Although the cocking handle is normally non-reciprocating, the F1 incorporates a device by which it can be made to engage the bolt. This means that if the mechanism becomes jammed with dirt the bolt can be worked backwards and forwards by means of the handle in order to loosen it. The pistol grip is a standard rifle component.

The Australian F1 sub-machine gun: note height of the shaped metal flap of the backsight.

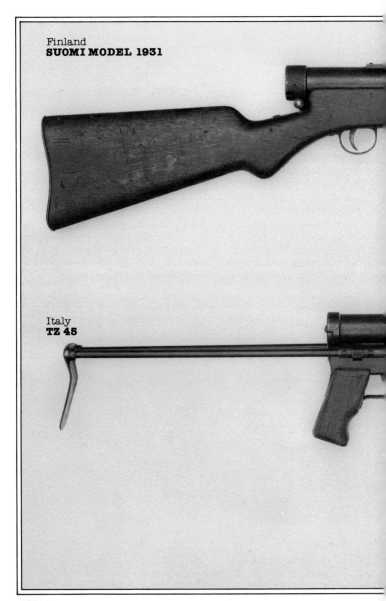

Finland
SUOMI MODEL 1931

Italy
TZ 45

SUOMI MODEL 1931

Length:	34·25" (870mm)
Weight:	10·34lb (4·69kg)
Barrel:	12·5" (317mm)
Calibre:	9mm
Rifling:	6 groove r/hand
Feed:	(See text)
C. Rate:	900 rpm
Muz Vel:	1312 f/s (400 m/s)
Sights:	110-547 yds

TZ 45

Length:	33·5" (851mm)
Weight:	7·20lb (3·26kg)
Barrel:	9" (229mm)
Calibre:	9mm
Rifling:	6 groove r/hand
Feed:	20/40-round box
C. Rate:	550 rpm
Muz Vel:	1250 f/s (365 m/s)
Sights:	Fixed

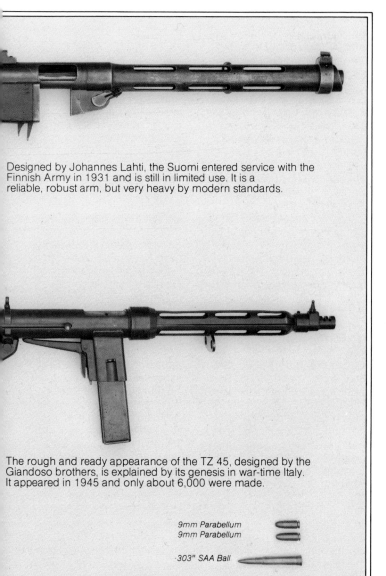

Designed by Johannes Lahti, the Suomi entered service with the
Finnish Army in 1931 and is still in limited use. It is a
reliable, robust arm, but very heavy by modern standards.

The rough and ready appearance of the TZ 45, designed by the
Giandoso brothers, is explained by its genesis in war-time Italy.
It appeared in 1945 and only about 6,000 were made.

9mm Parabellum
9mm Parabellum

·303" SAA Ball

Finland
SUOMI MODEL 1931

Suomi is the native word for Finland, and the first of the series bearing the name was developed from 1922 onwards which makes it one of the earliest sub-machine guns to appear. It was designed by the well-known Finnish designer Johannes Lahti, and the first finished models appeared in 1926. They were effective but very complex weapons, designed to fire the 7·62mm Parabellum cartridge from a magazine with such a pronounced curve that three of them placed end to end formed a complete circle. This gun was only produced in very small numbers and is thus chiefly of interest because it was the first of a series. The model illustrated was also designed by Lahti, but although it retained some of the features of the Model 26, so many changes were made that it was virtually a new weapon. Although patents were not finally granted until 1932 the gun was in use by the Finnish Army in the previous year, hence its final designation of Model 31. It worked by normal blowback system and had no less than four different magazines, a single 20-round box, a double 50-round box, and two drums, one of 40-round capacity and one of 71. Like most sub-machine guns of its vintage it was very well made of good steel, heavily machined and milled and unusually well finished. The end product was therefore an exceptionally reliable and robust weapon and although it was very heavy by modern standards (with the bigger drum magazine it weighed over fifteen pounds) this at least had the merit of reducing recoil and vibration and thus increasing its accuracy, for which it was very well known.

It was made under licence in Sweden, Denmark, and Switzerland, and apart from Finland was also used by Sweden, Switzerland and Norway and to a lesser extent Poland. It is still used in many units of the Finnish Army, although all surviving weapons have been modified to take a modern 36-round box magazine of improved pattern. At the end of 1939 the Russians, having failed to persuade the Finns to make some territorial adjustments to enhance Soviet security, invaded Finland. The Finns fought bravely and made good use of the Suomi.

A Finnish soldier fires his Suomi Model 1931 SMG; in this case fed from a drum magazine.

Italy
TZ 45

So many Italian sub-machine guns have been produced by the famous Brescian firm of Beretta that it sometimes comes as something of a surprise to people to find an Italian weapon of this type produced by some other firm. World War II, however, saw the appearance of a considerable variety of other weapons, the TZ 45 being amongst them. It was designed by the Giandoso brothers as a wartime expedient and first went into limited production in 1945. This new gun, which worked on the normal blowback system, was very crudely made and finished, partly of roughly machined parts and partly of stampings. This is not surprising in view of its date of manufacture, by which time the quality of most other countries' products had dropped

correspondingly. One of the interesting features of this gun is that it incorporates a grip safety; this consists of an L-shaped lever just behind the magazine housing (which also acts as a forward hand grip). Firm pressure on the vertical part of the lever (which is clearly visible in the photograph) causes the horizontal arm to be depressed sufficiently to withdraw an upper stud from the bolt way, thus allowing the working parts to function. This device which was similar to the one employed on some models of the Danish Madsen sub-machine gun, was a useful one, but it did of course prevent the weapon being used single-handed. The TZ 45 had a retractable stock, made of light tubing; when pushed in the front ends engaged in holes in a plate below the barrel about six inches (153mm) from the muzzle. Although probably not specifically intended for the

purpose it presumably also acted as a stop to prevent the weapon being pulled back from a port in an armoured vehicle by some sudden jolt, rather like the attachment on the German 'Schmeisser'. There are two parallel slots cut into the top of the barrel at the muzzle end which act as a crude but moderately effective compensator. Although it was an adequate weapon the TZ 45 came too late in the war to be of much use and only about six thousand were made. These were chiefly used by Italian troops on internal security duties including the rounding up of the armed deserters of half-a-dozen nationalities who had happily taken to banditry in the last months of the war. After the war the gun was offered commercially on the world market, but only the Burmese showed interest, a number being locally made there in the early 1950s. These guns were manu-factured under the title BA 52.

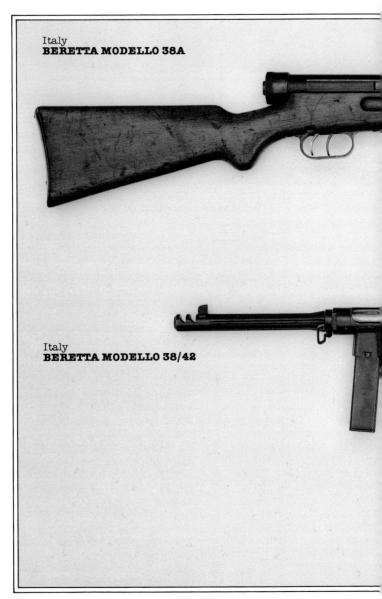

Italy
BERETTA MODELLO 38A

Italy
BERETTA MODELLO 38/42

BERETTA MODELLO 38A

Length:	37·25" (946mm)
Weight:	9·25lb (4·97kg)
Barrel:	12·4" (315mm)
Calibre:	9mm
Rifling:	6 groove r/hand
Feed:	10/20/40-round box
C. Rate:	600 rpm
Muz Vel:	1378 f/s (420 m/s)
Sights:	547 yds (500m)

BERETTA MODELLO 38/42

Length:	31·5" (800mm)
Weight:	7·20lb (3·26kg)
Barrel:	8·4" (216mm)
Calibre:	9mm
Rifling:	6 groove r/hand
Feed:	20/40-round box
C. Rate:	550 rpm
Muz Vel:	1250 f/s (381 m/s)
Sights:	219 yds (200m)

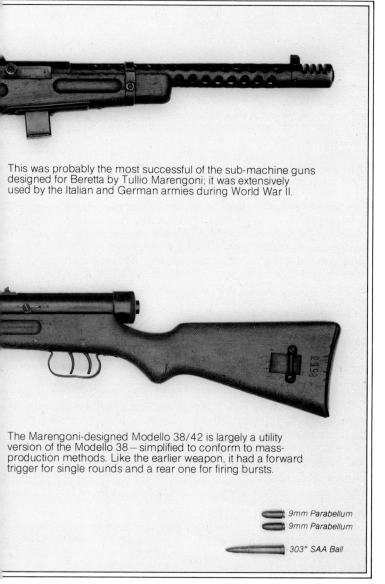

This was probably the most successful of the sub-machine guns designed for Beretta by Tullio Marengoni; it was extensively used by the Italian and German armies during World War II.

The Marengoni-designed Modello 38/42 is largely a utility version of the Modello 38 — simplified to conform to mass-production methods. Like the earlier weapon, it had a forward trigger for single rounds and a rear one for firing bursts.

9mm Parabellum

9mm Parabellum

·303" SAA Ball

Italy
BERETTA MODELLO 38A

The Northern Italian firm of
Beretta had a deservedly high
reputation for its sub-machine
guns, most of which have been
designed by their most talented
engineer, Tullio Marengoni,
who worked for them for many
years. Among the weapons he
produced was the Modello 38A
which probably has good claims
to be regarded as his most
successful sub-machine gun. It
had its origins in a self-loading
carbine which was first
produced in small numbers for
police use in 1935, but which
by 1938 had been improved to
the point where it could be
manufactured as a true sub-
machine gun. It came of
course far too early for the
mass-production techniques
developed a few years later and
was made to the high pre-war
standards customary among
gun makers. It was therefore
well machined and finished
which made it expensive to
produce, but which resulted in
a most reliable and accurate
arm. It functioned by normal
blowback and had a separate
firing pin, again a somewhat

unusual refinement. Its forward
trigger was for single shots, the
other for bursts. The first model
can be distinguised by the
elongated slots in its jacket,
by its compensator, which
consisted of a single large hole
in the top of the muzzle with a
bar across it, and by the fact
that it was fitted with a folding,
knife-type bayonet. Not many of
these were produced before
the elongated cooling slots
were replaced by round holes,
which thereafter remained
standard. The third version,
which is the one illustrated, was
mainly distinguished by the
absence of a bayonet and by its
new compensator consisting of
four separate cuts across the
muzzle. This version remained
as the production model for the
remainder of the war, although
there are some minor con-
cessions to the principles of
mass-production, notably in the
use of a pressed and welded
jacket. This version was used
extensively by both the Italian
and the German armies, and
captured specimens were
popular with Allied soldiers.
The Beretta Modello 38A was
also used by a number of
countries, notably Romania
and Argentina.

Italian soldiers during World War II, with slung Beretta Modello 38A sub-machine guns. The man on the left has in place on his weapon what appears to be the 20-round box magazine.

Italy
BERETTA MODELLO 38/42

After a year or so of war the Italians, like all other combatants, soon realized that they would have to accept modern mass-production methods if their supplies of war *matériel* were to keep pace with demand. As far as sub-machine guns were concerned, this realization resulted in the Beretta Modello 38/42, which like most of its predecessors was invented by Marengoni, and which came into full production in 1942. It was for all practical purposes a utility version of the earlier Modello 38, although it also incorporated a number of features from another sub-machine gun, the Modello 1, which had been designed, needless to say by Marengoni, in 1941 as a weapon for airborne forces on the lines of the German MP 40, but which had never gone into production due to its complicated construction. The whole weapon had also of course been considerably simplified to conform to modern mass-production methods, but in spite of this it was an efficient and popular gun. As far as external appearances were concerned there were a number of differences. The rifle-type stock, athough similar, was cut short at the magazine housing, and the adjustable rearsight disappeared, as did the perforated jacket which had been such a notable feature of many Beretta guns. The barrel had deep parallel fluting along its whole length, this being intended to assist the dissipation of heat in the absence of the jacket, while the compensator was reduced to two cuts only instead of the previous four. The bolt was somewhat simplified with a fixed firing pin integral with it instead of the separate mechanism previously used. The main return spring worked on a rod, the end of which extended appreciably beyond the rear of the receiver, and as before the gun had two triggers, the forward one for single rounds, the rear one for bursts. The cocking handle, which does not move with the bolt, had a dust cover attached to it to keep the internal mechanism as clear as possible. The general appearance of the gun was utilitarian as compared with its predecessors, stampings and welding having been used wherever possible, although the finish was surprisingly good and the whole weapon strong and serviceable. Later productions had plain barrels instead of the distinctive fluted ones and were sometimes referred to as the Modello 38/44. There was a later variation still, in which the weight and dimensions of the bolt were reduced; this led in turn to a somewhat shorter return spring and rod, which did not protrude beyond the rear of the receiver as in the earlier models. The date that this model went into production is not very clear, but most of them seem to have come off the assembly lines after the end of the war so that its designation 38/44 is somewhat in doubt. The Beretta 38/42 was widely used by the Italians and Germans and after the war a number of the 38/44 Model were sold to various countries including Syria and Pakistan.

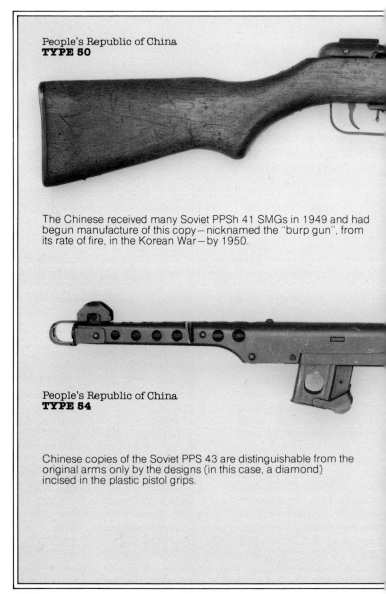

People's Republic of China
TYPE 50

The Chinese received many Soviet PPSh 41 SMGs in 1949 and had begun manufacture of this copy—nicknamed the "burp gun", from its rate of fire, in the Korean War—by 1950.

People's Republic of China
TYPE 54

Chinese copies of the Soviet PPS 43 are distinguishable from the original arms only by the designs (in this case, a diamond) incised in the plastic pistol grips.

TYPE 50

Length:	33·75" (858mm)
Weight:	8lb (3·63kg)
Barrel:	10·75" (273mm)
Calibre:	7·62mm
Rifling:	4 groove r/hand
Feed:	35-round box
C. Rate:	900 rpm
Muz Vel:	1400 f/s (472 m/s)
Sights:	110-219 yds

TYPE 54

Length:	32·25" (819mm)
Weight:	7·4lb (3·36kg)
Barrel:	10" (254mm)
Calibre:	7·62mm
Rifling:	4 groove r/hand
Feed:	35-round box
C. Rate:	700 rpm
Muz Vel:	1600 f/s (488 m/s)
Sights:	Flip, 110-219 yds

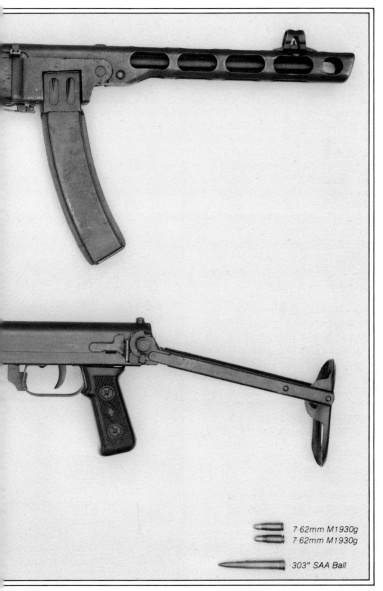

7·62mm M1930g
7·62mm M1930g

·303" SAA Ball

People's Republic of China
TYPE 50

Like many of the weapons used by Communist China, their sub-machine gun Type 50 had its origins in a weapon first produced by the Soviet Union, in this case the PPSh 41.
As with most other combatant nations the Russians soon saw the need for mass production and the new gun was largely made of heavy gauge stampings, welded, pinned and brazed as necessary. The gun was of normal blowback mechanism and had the interior of the barrel chromed, a fairly common Soviet device. One of its distinctive features is that the front end of the perforated barrel casing slopes steeply backward from top to bottom, thus acting as a compensator to keep the muzzle down. In spite of its high cyclic rate of fire the gun was reasonably accurate and could be fired in single rounds if required. The earliest versions had a tangent backsight but this was soon replaced by a simpler flip sight. The Chinese Communists received many of these guns in and after 1949 and started their own large scale manufacture of them in 1949 or 1950. Their version was essentially similar to its Russian counterpart, but had a somewhat lighter stock. It is also designed to take a curved box magazine though it will also fire the 71-round drum which was the standard magazine on the original Russian model. All Chinese versions have the two-range flip sight. The first locally-made weapons were crude in the extreme and gave the impression of having been made by apprentice blacksmiths (as perhaps they

were). Nevertheless they worked, which was the first and only requirement of the Chinese. The Type 50 was used extensively by the Chinese in the Korean war where it earned the inelegant but expressive nickname 'burp-gun' from its high rate of fire. Many were also used against the French in Indo-China in the 1950s.

People's Republic of China
TYPE 54

The origins of this particular weapon are unusual, since it was designed by A. Sudarev at Leningrad in 1942 when the city was under actual blockade by the Germans. Arms were in short supply and as none could be brought in it became necessary to improvise from local resources. The new gun originally known as the Russian PPS 42, was therefore made in the city itself, so that weapons coming off the production line

were liable to be used in action in a matter of hours. As was to be expected the gun was made of stampings, using any suitable grade of metal, and was held together by riveting, welding, and pinning. Nevertheless it was not only cheap but it turned out to be effective. It worked on the usual simple blowback system and would only fire automatic; perhaps its oddest feature was its semi-circular compensator, which helped to keep the muzzle down but increased blast considerably. This was followed by the PPS 43, modified and improved by the same engineer who had been responsible for the earlier model. Its most unusual feature was that it had no separate ejector in the normal sense of the word. The bolt moved backwards and forwards along a guide rod which was of such a length that as the bolt came back with the empty case, the end of the rod

caught it a sharp blow and knocked it clear.

After the Chinese revolution of 1949, the Soviet Union naturally supplied its new ally with a considerable quantity of arms including large numbers of the PPS 43, and by 1953 the Chinese had begun large-scale manufacture of these weapons, virtually unchanged in appearance from the Russian prototypes. The only way in which it can be distinguished is by the fact that the plastic pistol grips often bear a large letter K in a central design. This, however, is by no means universal and other designs, including a diamond, may be found. The gun is still often found in South East Asia.

A soldier of the People's Republic of China receives instruction in the 7·62mm Type 54 sub-machine gun, a direct copy of the Soviet PPS 43. The Chinese lay great emphasis on aquatic training; hence this unusual firing position.

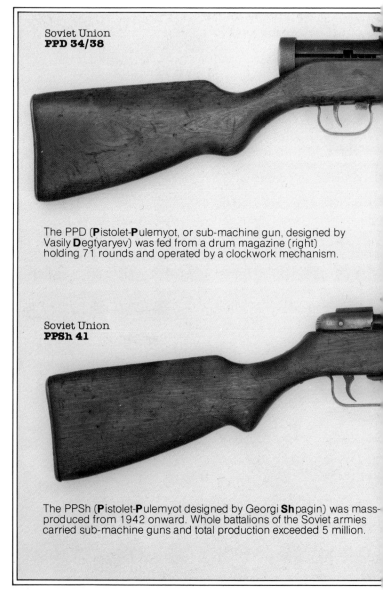

Soviet Union
PPD 34/38

The PPD (**P**istolet-**P**ulemyot, or sub-machine gun, designed by
Vasily **D**egtyaryev) was fed from a drum magazine (right)
holding 71 rounds and operated by a clockwork mechanism.

Soviet Union
PPSh 41

The PPSh (**P**istolet-**P**ulemyot designed by Georgi **Sh**pagin) was mass-
produced from 1942 onward. Whole battalions of the Soviet armies
carried sub-machine guns and total production exceeded 5 million.

PPD 34/38

Length	30·6" (779mm)
Weight:	8·25lb (3·74kg)
Barrel:	10·75" (272mm)
Calibre:	7·62mm
Rifling:	4 groove r/hand
Feed:	71-round drum
C. Rate:	800 rpm
Muz Vel:	1600 f/s (489 m/s)
Sights:	547 yds (500m)

PPSh 41

Length:	33·1" (841mm)
Weight:	8·0lb (3·63kg)
Barrel	10·6" (269mm)
Calibre:	7·62mm
Rifling:	4 groove r/hand
Feed:	71 drum/35 box
C. Rate:	900 rpm
Muz Vel:	1600 f/s (489 m/s)
Sights:	547 yds (500m)

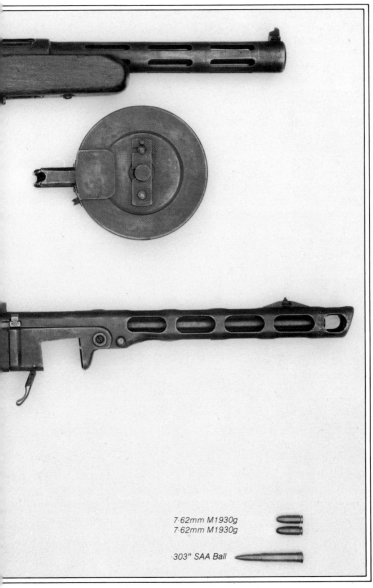

7·62mm M1930g
7·62mm M1930g

·303" SAA Ball

Soviet Union
PPD 34/38

This weapon was designed by Vasily Degtyaryev, the well-known Soviet expert on automatic weapons, and the D in the title is his initial, the PP standing for Pistolet-Pulemyot, the usual Russian term for what we know as a sub-machine gun. It initially appeared in 1934 and may be regarded as the first really successful weapon of its type to be used in the Soviet Army.

It was based fairly closely on the German MP28.II, and coming before the days of mass-production was reasonably well made and finished by the standards of Russian industry as it then was. The PPD worked by normal blowback on the open bolt principle single rounds or bursts being obtained by the use of a selector in front of the trigger. Both bore and chamber were chromed to prevent undue wear. The cartridges were fed from a near-vertical drum with an unusual extension piece which fitted into the bottom of the receiver; this drum, which was worked by clockwork, was very similar mechanically to that of the Finnish Suomi, and held seventy-one rounds. This gave the soldier using it a good reserve of fire without having to reload, but made the gun heavy. As drum magazines are susceptible to dirt, there were probably also problems over stoppages; there was in fact also a curved box magazine but this was very rarely used. One or two minor variations to the original model were made, the most obvious being the reduction in the number of jacket slots from rows of eight small ones to three larger ones. Although the gun was technically replaced by the PPD 40 in 1940 it was used in the Finnish campaigns and probably also saw later service elsewhere.

Red Army soldiers with a knocked-out German AFV during World War II. Those at centre and right have PPD 34/38 sub-machine guns.

Tank-mounted Russian scouts with PPSh 41 sub-machine guns; note that these have drum magazines.

Soviet Union
PPSh 41

At the outbreak of World War II in 1939, the Soviet Army was armed with the PPD 34/38, but by the beginning of 1940 this was gradually being replaced by a modified version of the PPD 40 which was similar in appearance but took a different type of drum. Almost immediately the gun illustrated was put into limited production, and after stringent testing by the Russian Army was finally approved early in 1942, after which production was on a vast scale. It was designed by Georgii Shpagin, another well-known Russian expert, and this fact is denoted by the inclusion of his initial in the official designation of the new gun. The PPSh was an early and successful example of the application of mass-production techniques to the manufacture of firearms, a change made essential by the Soviet Union's huge military commitments at that time. As far as possible it was made from sheet metal stampings, welding and riveting being used wherever feasible, and although it retained the rather old-fashioned looking wooden butt it was a sturdy and reliable arm. It worked on the usual blowback system with a buffer at the rear end of the receiver to reduce vibration and had a selector lever in front of the trigger to give single rounds or burst as required. As its cyclic rate of fire was high and would have tended to make the muzzle rise when firing bursts, the front of the barrel jacket was sloped backwards so as to act as a compensator, a simple and reasonably successful expedient. Feed for the PPSh was either by a seventy-one round drum, basically similar to that of the earlier PPD series but not interchangeable with them, or by a thirty-five round box. In order to reduce wear and help cleaning, the bore and chamber of these guns were all chromed. There appear to have been only two basic models of this gun; the first model, the one illustrated, had a somewhat complicated tangent backsight, while the second one made do with a perfectly adequate two aperture flip sight. The Soviet armies greatly favoured the sub-machine gun and on occasions whole battalions were armed with it, so it is not surprising that the total numbers manufactured should have exceeded five million. It was also widely copied by other Communist countries, and although long obsolete in the Soviet Union itself it is probably still extensively used elsewhere. The Chinese in particular copied it as their Type 50 and must themselves have produced it in vast numbers.

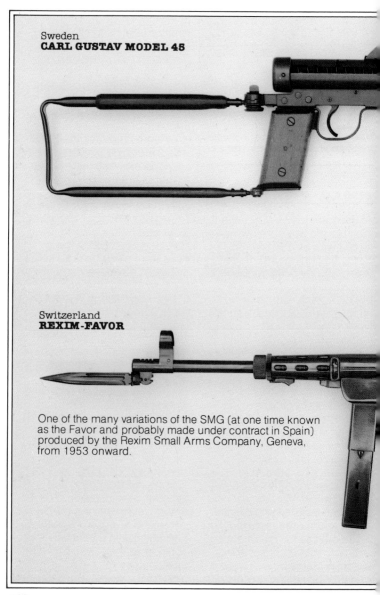

Sweden
CARL GUSTAV MODEL 45

Switzerland
REXIM-FAVOR

One of the many variations of the SMG (at one time known as the Favor and probably made under contract in Spain) produced by the Rexim Small Arms Company, Geneva, from 1953 onward.

CARL GUSTAV MODEL 45

Length:	31·8″ (808mm)
Weight	7·62lb (3·45kg)
Barrel:	8·0″ (203mm)
Calibre:	9mm
Rifling:	6 groove r/hand
Feed:	36/50-round box
C. Rate:	600 rpm
Muz Vel:	1210 f/s (369 m/s)
Sights:	328 yds (300m)

REXIM-FAVOR

Length:	32·0″ (813mm)
Weight	7·0lb (3·18kg)
Barrel:	10·75″ (273mm)
Calibre:	9mm
Rifling:	5 groove r/hand
Feed:	20-round box
C. Rate:	600 rpm
Muz Vel:	1300 f/s (396 m/s)
Sights:	Flip. 100/200 yds

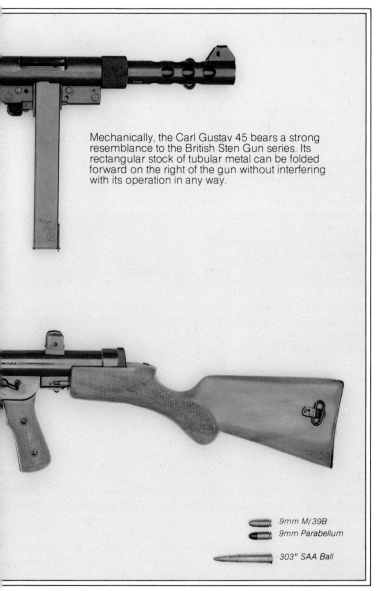

Mechanically, the Carl Gustav 45 bears a strong resemblance to the British Sten Gun series. Its rectangular stock of tubular metal can be folded forward on the right of the gun without interfering with its operation in any way.

9mm M/39B

9mm Parabellum

·303″ SAA Ball

Sweden
CARL GUSTAV MODEL 45

Sweden did not adopt a sub-machine gun until 1937, when she began to manufacture a slightly modified form of the Finnish Suomi, which was made under licence by the Carl Gustav factory. This was replaced soon afterwards by a second version of the same gun, which had a shorter barrel, a very large trigger guard, which could accommodate gloved fingers in winter, and a much straighter stock than the original Finnish gun; this gun was made by the firm of Husqvarna. In the course of World War II Sweden, although neutral, increased her army considerably to defend herself if necessary and this led to the realization that she had no simple sub-machine gun for mass-production. She set out to rectify this but the result, the Model 1945, was not in fact put into production until after the war. The Model 1945 was made of stampings from heavy gauge steel, riveted or welded as necessary, and within the limits imposed by these methods was a sound and reliable weapon.

Mechanically it bore a strong resemblance to the British Sten gun, but had a rectangular stock of tubular metal which could be folded forward on the right of the gun without in any way interfering with its working. Although it was designed for firing on automatic only, single rounds could be fired by anyone with a reasonably sensitive trigger finger. It fired a special high velocity cartridge, and the original model used the old Suomi fifty-round magazine. Later versions fired a new thirty-six round type but as large stocks of the older

magazine, which was not interchangeable, remained, the new gun had an easily detached magazine housing which could be replaced by one of the older type if required. This was a temporary provision only until adequate supplies of the new magazine became available, and the latest models have riveted magazine housings.

Above: *Swedish soldier with slung Carl Gustav Model 45 SMG; tubular stock folded forward.*

Left: *The 9mm Carl Gustav 45 is held in the firing position.*

Switzerland
REXIM-FAVOR

The history of this weapon is somewhat obscure. It was presented by the Turkish Army, attractively cased with a variety of accessories, to a senior British service officer attending an international rifle meeting in 1968. The Turks are not known to make sub-machine guns and there is no reason to suppose that it was locally made. The various inscriptions on the change lever and elsewhere are in the Turkish language but there is little doubt that it is one of the many varieties of the Swiss Rexim sub-machine gun which appeared from 1953 onwards, under the auspices of the Rexim Small Arms Company located in Geneva. It was at one time known as the Favor sub-machine gun, and is believed to have been made under contract by the Spanish Arsenal at Corunna. Extensive attempts were made in the mid-1950s to sell the Rexim in the Middle East, but there seems to be no record of any substantial deals being made, principally because the gun was considered to be too complicated, never a good recommendation for a sub-machine gun in which simplicity is almost the most important factor. The chief interest of the Rexim was that it fired from a closed bolt, that is, the round was fed into the chamber by the action of the cocking handle and remained there until pressure on the trigger allowed the firing pin to go forward. Motive power was provided by two coiled springs, one working inside the other with an intermediate hollow hammer, and looking exactly like an old-fashioned three-draw telescope. When the trigger was pressed the depression of the sear released the hammer which went forward under the force of the large outer spring, struck the firing pin, and fired the round. Normal blowback then followed and the cycle continued. The gun was well made, chiefly of pressings, but with a superior finish. It had a quick release barrel, in which the withdrawal of the small catch under the milled nut allowed the nut to be unscrewed and the barrel pulled out forward. In the model illustrated the butt had a separate pistol grip, presumably designed as a rear hand grip when using the short spring bayonet permanently attached to the muzzle. It took a magazine identical with that of the German MP40 gun. The gun illustrated is probably one of a small number purchased at some time by Turkey but never adopted for service.

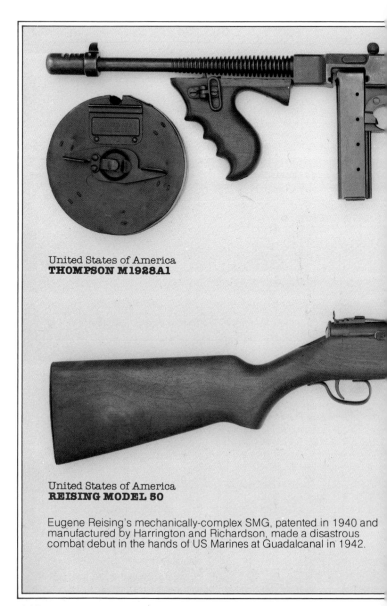

United States of America
THOMPSON M1928A1

United States of America
REISING MODEL 50

Eugene Reising's mechanically-complex SMG, patented in 1940 and manufactured by Harrington and Richardson, made a disastrous combat debut in the hands of US Marines at Guadalcanal in 1942.

THOMPSON M1928A1

Length:	33.75" (857mm)
Weight:	10.75lb (4.88kg)
Barrel:	10.5" (267mm)
Calibre:	.45"
Rifling:	6 groove r/hand
Feed:	50 drum/20 box
C. Rate:	800 rpm
Muz Vel:	920 f/s (281 m/s)
Sights:	600 yds (549m)

REISING MODEL 50

Length:	35.75" (908mm)
Weight:	6.75lb (3.06kg)
Barrel:	11.0" (279mm)
Calibre:	.45"
Rifling:	6 groove r/hand
Feed:	12- or 20-round box
C. Rate:	550 rpm
Muz Vel:	920 f/s (280 m/s)
Sights:	300 yds (274m)

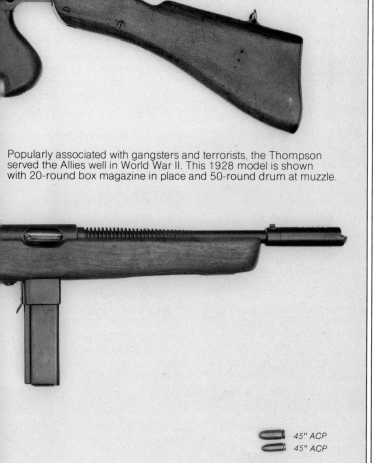

Popularly associated with gangsters and terrorists, the Thompson
served the Allies well in World War II. This 1928 model is shown
with 20-round box magazine in place and 50-round drum at muzzle.

.45" ACP

.45" ACP

.303" SAA Ball

A British Army lance-corporal fires a Thompson M1928A1 sub-machine gun from the hip. A few of these US-designed arms were made by BSA.

United States of America
THOMPSON M1928A1

Some mention has already been made of the Thompson sub-machine gun in the introduction to this section, since it was in many ways the most famous of all weapons of its type. It was developed in the course of World War I by Colonel (later Brigadier-General) J. T. Thompson but came too late to be used in action. Very few people wanted sub-machine guns after the war had ended so that the Auto-Ordnance Corporation which made them found it very difficult to keep going, particularly in the depression of the 1930s. Good advertising and publicity helped, however, and there was a small but steady sale to law enforcement agencies and also, regrettably but unavoidably, to criminals of various types. A surprising variety of models of the Thompson were made, almost all in ·45″ calibre and one or two as automatic rifles rather than sub-machine guns. A few were even made in England by

the Birmingham Small Arms Company. The weapon illustrated is the 1928, which with minor changes was the last peacetime version. The gun worked by the usual blowback system, but somewhat unusually in guns of this description it had a delay device to prevent the bolt from opening until the barrel pressure had dropped. Two squared grooves were cut into the sides of the bolt at an angle of 45°, the lower ends being nearer the face of the bolt, and an H-shaped bridge fitted into these. When the bolt was fully home the bottom ends of the H-piece engaged in recesses in the receiver. When the cartridge fired, the pressure was enough to cause it to rise, thus allowing the bolt to go back after a brief delay. This was hardly necessary in terms of safety but had the useful effect of slowing the cyclic rate which assisted accurate firing. The gun took either a fifty-round drum or a twenty-round box magazine, both of which are shown in the illustration above. A few of the guns may still be used by some US police forces.

US soldiers — one in the foreground with a Thompson M1928A1, without forward pistol grip — hunt German stragglers in Luxembourg, 1945.

United States of America
REISING MODEL 50

The success of the sub-machine gun in the Spanish Civil War caused a good many arms designers to turn their attention to weapons of this type. One of those who did so was Eugene Reising who produced the weapon named after him in 1938; after incorporating some improvements he patented it in 1940 and the well-known United States arms firm of Harrington and Richardson began the manufacture of it at the end of the next year. After several tests had led to minor improvements in the gun, it was accepted for service by the United States Marine Corps and was first used in action on Guadalcanal where it proved to be a complete failure, jamming so frequently that the exasperated Marines, who were fighting desperately, threw it away in disgust and resorted to more reliable weapons. The causes of this were due principally to the complexity of the mechanism and its susceptibility to dirt. Most unusually, and quite unnecessarily, the gun fired with the breech locked, this being achieved by the action of a ramp which raised the rear of the bolt into a recess in the top of the receiver after the moment of firing. This would have been quite acceptable if there had been some self-clearing device, but as it was, the bolt recess soon filled with dirt, particularly in hot, dry climates, which effectively rendered the weapon useless. An odd feature of the Reising was that it had no cocking handle, this action being achieved by means of a finger catch at the bottom of the stock a few inches in front of the magazine. It is believed that the British Purchasing Commission bought a small number for Canada and the Soviet Union, but neither of the two countries appear to have left any opinion on record. In spite of its complexity the gun had good points and would probably have performed well in a reasonably temperate climate, perhaps as a weapon for police or other internal security forces.

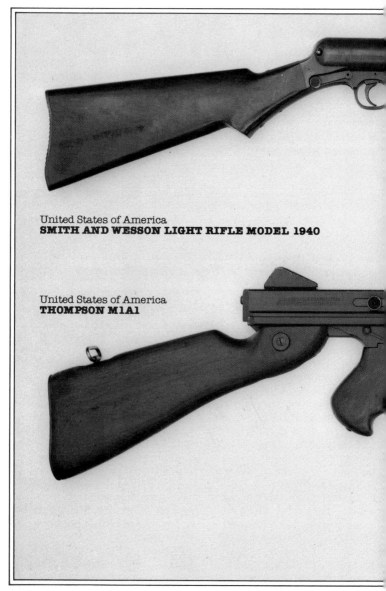

United States of America
SMITH AND WESSON LIGHT RIFLE MODEL 1940

United States of America
THOMPSON M1A1

SMITH AND WESSON
LIGHT RIFLE MODEL 1940

Length:	32·5″ (825mm)
Weight:	8·0lb (3·63kg)
Barrel:	8·5″ (216mm)
Calibre:	9mm
Rifling:	5 groove r/hand
Feed:	20-round box
Muz Vel:	1300 f/s (396 m/s)
Sights:	Fixed

THOMPSON M1A1

Length:	32·0″ (813mm)
Weight	10·45lb (4·74kg)
Barrel:	10·5″ (267mm)
Calibre:	·45″
Rifling:	6 groove r/hand
Feed:	20/30-round box
C. Rate:	700 rpm
Muz Vel:	920 f/s (281 m/s)
Sights:	109 yds (100m)

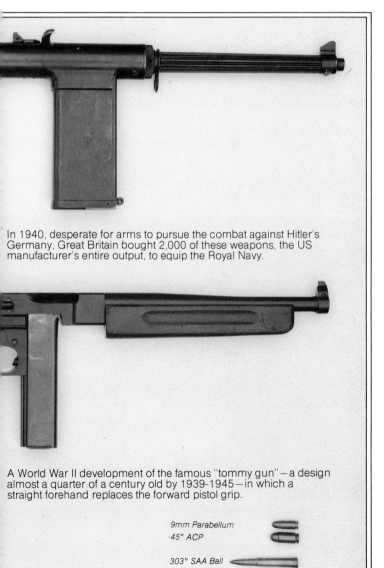

In 1940, desperate for arms to pursue the combat against Hitler's Germany, Great Britain bought 2,000 of these weapons, the US manufacturer's entire output, to equip the Royal Navy.

A World War II development of the famous "tommy gun" — a design almost a quarter of a century old by 1939-1945 — in which a straight forehand replaces the forward pistol grip.

9mm Parabellum
·45″ ACP

·303″ SAA Ball

United States of America
SMITH AND WESSON LIGHT RIFLE MODEL 1940

This weapon, which is believed to have been invented by a designer named Edward Pomeroy, was made in small numbers just before the outbreak of World War II by the famous American firm of Smith and Wesson. One of them was tested at the United States Army Proving Grounds at the end of the same year but was rejected, partly because it fired a 9mm round whereas the American Army favoured ·45″ and partly because it was only semi-automatic. Smith and Wesson were advised to convert it to a full automatic weapon in the larger calibre and re-submit it, but there is no record that they did so. It is said that a few of the original prototypes were made to fire automatic, which marginally justifies its inclusion as a sub-machine gun, but if so they were never tested, probably because Smith and Wesson had enough war work on their hands at the time. A slightly modified version of the type illustrated was in fact re-issued in 1940, when Great Britain, desperate for arms, bought the whole batch of two thousand for the Royal Navy, all the tools and gauges being forwarded with the order. The main thing that strikes one about this weapon is its quality; the bolt and barrel were made of chrome nickel steel, the remainder of the metalwork being of manganese steel, and the machining, blueing and general finishing are fully up to the peacetime standards expected of such a famous firm. It worked on the usual blowback system and fired from the open bolt position. One of its unusual features was that the back of the very wide magazine housing contained an ejector tube down which the empty cases passed after firing. In view of the small numbers made, specimens of this gun are very rare and much sought after. Official records of it are scarce and its history obscure.

United States of America
THOMPSON M1A1

The real breakthrough for the Thompson sub-machine gun came in 1938 when it was adopted by the United States Army. It was somewhat out of date and there were better weapons in existence but the Thompson was available and therefore accepted. Then the war came and the demand rose instantly. Apart from the domestic needs of the United States the main external purchaser was Great Britain who was glad enough to buy as many as she could be provided with in 1940. As with most other pre-war weapons the Thompson had been relatively luxuriously made, and in view of the need to speed up production some simplification became essential. The first result was the M1 Type, the main mechanical difference being the abolition of the H-piece and the substitution of a heavier bolt to compensate for it. The main external differences were the absence of the compensator on the muzzle, the substitution of a straight forehand for the forward pistol grip (although this had been optional on the Model 28), the removal of the rather complex backsight, and its replacement by a simple flip. One main difference in functioning was that the new gun would not take the fifty-round drum, but as this had never been very reliable in dirty conditions it was no loss. A new thirty-round box magazine was introduced at the same time, and the earlier twenty-round magazine would also fit the new model. There was yet another simplification, the incorporation of a fixed firing pin on the face of the bolt; this resulted in the M1A1 which is the weapon illustrated.

Although almost a quarter of a century old by then, the Thompson gave excellent service in 1939-45, for even if it was heavy to carry it was reliable, and its bullets had very considerable stopping power.

Above: *US Marine armed with Thompson M1A1 lands from an Amtrac at Okinawa, April 1945.*

Left: *British corporal fires his M1A1 from cover in the ruins of Cassino, March 1944.*

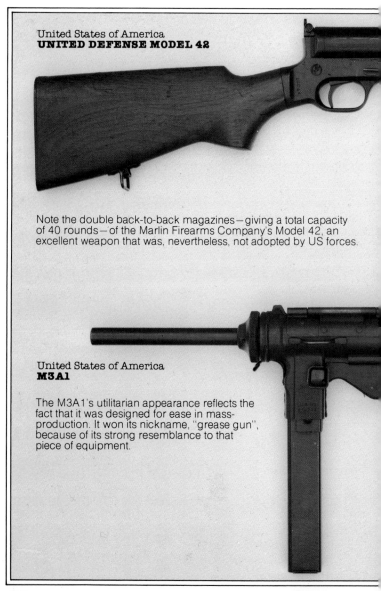

United States of America
UNITED DEFENSE MODEL 42

Note the double back-to-back magazines—giving a total capacity of 40 rounds—of the Marlin Firearms Company's Model 42, an excellent weapon that was, nevertheless, not adopted by US forces.

United States of America
M3A1

The M3A1's utilitarian appearance reflects the fact that it was designed for ease in mass-production. It won its nickname, "grease gun", because of its strong resemblance to that piece of equipment.

UNITED DEFENSE MODEL 42

Length:	32·3" (820mm)
Weight:	9·12lb (4·14kg)
Barrel:	11·0" (279mm)
Calibre:	9mm/·45"
Rifling:	6 groove r/hand
Feed:	20-round box
C. Rate:	700 rpm
Muz Vel:	1312 f/s (400 m/s)
Sights:	Fixed

M3A1

Length:	29·8" (757mm)
Weight:	8·15lb (3·70kg)
Barrel:	8·0" (203mm)
Calibre:	·45"
Rifling:	4 groove r/hand
Feed:	30-round box
C. Rate:	400 rpm
Muz Vel:	920 f/s (280 m/s)
Sights:	Fixed

9mm Parabellum

·45" ACP

·303" SAA Ball

United States of America
UNITED DEFENSE
MODEL 42

The United States Defense Supply Corporation was a United States Government corporation which was formed in 1941 to supply weapons to the various Allied nations involved in World War II. The first weapon it submitted for trial was a rather odd one with interchangeable barrels, one of 9mm and the other of ·45″, the barrel not actually being used for its proper function being screwed to the back of the receiver to act as a butt. This gun was a failure and never went into production. The UDM42, the sub-machine gun illustrated, was actually designed in about 1938 by a Carl Swebilius and was manufactured by the well-known Marlin Firearms Company. The Model 42 was of normal blowback operation with a separate firing pin inside the bolt, and after one or two modifications it performed particularly well, being accurate, easy to handle, and almost impervious to dirt. The original models were of ·45″ calibre and took a twenty-round box magazine, but the production models were all of 9mm and were fitted with double back-to-back magazines, with a total capacity of forty rounds.

The gun was probably one of the best to have been produced in the United States at that period. It was of the pre-war style of manufacture, made of machined steel and very well finished, but its main problem was that it came at a time when the United States already seemed to be well-equipped with sub-machine guns, as simplified wartime versions of the Thompson were available in production quantities. Perhaps even more important was the fact that the mass-produced M3 gun was in an advanced state of preparation and once that became available guns of pre-war quality and finish largely disappeared from the scene. It was a sad end for an excellent gun.

Above: *Among the weapons being examined by this Pathet Lao soldier are three US-made M3A1 "grease guns" (rear of row).*

Right: *USMC corporal in training; with M3A1 slung.*

United States of America
M3A1

In 1941 the Small Arms Development Branch of the United States Army Ordnance Corps set out to develop a sub-machine gun in accordance with certain guidelines proposed by the various combat arms. The intention was to produce a weapon which could be mass-produced by modern methods, and once the basic design had been established by George Hyde, a well-known expert in the field of sub-machine guns, the production side was put into the hands of Frederick Sampson, an expert of equal standing in his own field. A very detailed study of the methods used to manufacture the successful British Sten gun was also made, and the work went ahead so quickly that prototypes had been successfully tested well before the end of 1942, and the new weapon accepted as standard under the designation of M3.

The new gun was a very utilitarian looking arm, made as far as possible from stampings and with practically no machining except for the barrel and bolt. It worked by blowback and had no provision for firing single rounds, but as its cyclic rate was low this was acceptable. Its stock was of retractable wire and the calibre was ·45" although conversion to 9mm was not difficult. It bore a strong resemblance to a grease gun, from which it derived its famous nickname. Large-scale use revealed some defects in the gun, and further successful attempts to simplify it were initiated; these resulted in the M3A1 which is the weapon here illustrated. Like its predecessor the new gun was made by modern methods and was generally reliable. It worked, as before, by blowback but had no cocking handle, this process being achieved by the insertion of a finger into a slot cut in the receiver, by which the bolt could be withdrawn. The bolt, which had an integral firing pin, worked on guide rods which saved complicated finishing of the inside of the receiver and which gave smooth functioning with little interruption from dirt. An oil container was built into the pistol grip and a small bracket added to the rear of the retractable butt acted as a magazine filler. It used a box magazine which was not altogether reliable in dirty or dusty conditions until the addition of an easily removed plastic cover eliminated this defect. By the end of 1944 the new gun had been adopted and three months later it had officially replaced the Thompson as the standard sub-machine gun of the United States Army.

Picture Credits

Unless otherwise credited, all pictures in this book were taken by Bruce Scott in the Weapons Museum, British School of Infantry, Warminster, Wiltshire.

The publisher wishes to thank the following organizations and individuals who have supplied photographs for this book. Photographs have been credited by page number; where more than one photograph appears on a page, references are made in the order of the columns across the page and then from top to bottom. The following abbreviations have been used: Bentham Literary Services (Colonel John Weeks): BLS; Imperial War Museum: IWM; Military Archive & Research Service, London: MARS.

6-7: US Army; 8: US Army; 9: BLS; 10: Novosti Press Agency; 10-11: BLS; 12: E and TV Films, London/US Army; 13: Popperfoto; 15: IWM; 18-19: NATO; 27: Terry Gander (2); 30-31: MARS; 34: IWM; 38: IWM; 42-43: IWM/Terry Gander/IWM; 44-45: IWM/Central Office of Information, London; 48-49: MoD, London (Peter Stevenson)/ Terry Gander; 52: National Archives, Washington; 56: US Army; 60-61: US Army; 65: MARS; 68-69: IWM; 72-73: MARS/Terry Gander (2); 74: IWM (2); 75: US Army; 78-79: US Army/NATO/IWM; 80-81: Central Office of Information, London; 82-83: BLS; 84-85: IWM/US Signal Corps; 88: IWM/Sipho SA (Will Fowler Collection); 89: UPI (Will Fowler Collection); 93: Terry Gander; 96-97: MARS (2); 100: IWM; 101: Terry Gander; 105: Terry Gander/US Army; 108-109: Terry Gander (2); 112: IWM; 113: Terry Gander; 116-117: Terry Gander (2); 120-121: BSA (2); 124: Central Office of Information, London; 125: Terry Gander; 129: Terry Gander; 132: Beretta; 140: Terry Gander; 141: IWM; 144: Terry Gander; 145: MARS; 148: Terry Gander; 149: IWM; 152-153: IWM/MARS; 156-157: US Army/US Marine Corps.

Bibliography

Weapons general		Place and year of publication	
Jane's Infantry Weapons	Weeks (Ed)	London	1979
Military Small Arms of the 20th Century	Hogg and Weeks	London	1977
Brasseys Infantry Weapons of the World	Owen (Ed)	London	1975
Small Arms of the World	Smith	London	1973
Illustrated Arsenal of the Third Reich	Normount	Wichenburg Arizona	1973
Arms and Armament	ffoulkes	London	1945
The Soldier's Trade	Myatt	London	1974
British and American Infantry Weapons of World War II	Barker	London	1969
German Infantry Weapons of World War II	Barker	London	1969
Pistols, Rifles and Machine Guns	Allen	London	1953
Superiority of Fire	Pridham	London	1945
Small Arms Operation and Identification of Small Arms	Johnson (US Army Publication)	USA	1976
NATO Infantry and its Weapons	Owen (Ed)	London	1976
Warsaw Pact Infantry and its Weapons	Owen (Ed)	London	1976
Text-book for Small Arms	HMSO	London	1919
Text-book for Small Arms	HMSO	London	1929
Text-book of Ammunition	HMSO	London	1926

Note: Much use has been made of a variety of British and Foreign Military textbooks and pamphlets held in the Weapons Museum Reference Library, Warminster.

Sub-machine Guns			
The World's Sub-machine Guns	Nelson/Lockoven	London	1977
Pictorial History of the Sub-machine Gun	Hobart	London	1973

Rifles			
The Book of the Rifle	Fremantle	London	1901
The Englishman and the Rifle	Cottesloe	London	1945
The Book of Rifles	Smith	Harrisburgh Pa	1965
The Lee-Enfield Rifle	Reynolds	London	1960
Remarks on the Rifle (11th Ed)	Baker	London	1935
English Guns and Rifles	George	London	1947

GUIDES IN THIS SERIES...........

AN ILLUSTRATED GUIDE TO
ALLIED FIGHTERS OF WORLD WAR II
160 fact-packed pages in colour. Descriptions of over 40 aircraft types, plus many variants
Over 110 photographs, many in colour. More than 130 detailed line drawings. Over 50 colour drawings
Bill Gunston

AN ILLUSTRATED GUIDE TO
WORLD WAR II TANKS AND FIGHTING VEHICLES
39 formidable tanks and many variants described in 160 fact-packed pages in colour
More than 170 superb illustrations, including action photographs and highly detailed colour drawings
Edited by Christopher F. Foss

AN ILLUSTRATED GUIDE TO
RIFLES AND SUB-MACHINE GUNS
43 modern rifles and 55 sub-machine guns. All photographed in full colour. 35,000 words of text
Major Frederick Myatt M.C.

AN ILLUSTRATED GUIDE TO
GERMAN, ITALIAN AND JAPANESE FIGHTERS OF WORLD WAR II
Major Fighters and Attack Aircraft of the Axis Powers
160 fact-packed pages in colour. Descriptions of well over 50 aircraft types, plus many variants
120 dramatic photographs, many in colour. More than 180 detailed line drawings. Over 50 colour drawings
Bill Gunston

AN ILLUSTRATED GUIDE TO
BOMBERS OF WORLD WAR II
160 fact-packed pages in colour. Descriptions of well over 50 aircraft types, plus many variants
More than 140 detailed line drawings. 90 dramatic photographs, many in colour. Over 40 colour drawings
Bill Gunston

AN ILLUSTRATED GUIDE TO
MODERN FIGHTERS AND ATTACK AIRCRAFT
Fact-packed descriptions of 60 of the world's most exciting warplanes
120 action photographs most in full colour. 180 line drawings. 34 superb colour profiles
Bill Gunston

AN ILLUSTRATED GUIDE TO
MODERN TANKS AND FIGHTING VEHICLES
The world's major combat vehicles described in 160 fact-packed pages
120 action photographs, most in colour. Superbly detailed technical drawings
Edited by Ray Bonds

AN ILLUSTRATED GUIDE TO
MODERN WARSHIPS
Over 60 of the world's most exciting warships
160 fact-packed pages in colour. 130 action photographs. Over 60 technical drawings
Hugh Lyon

* Each has 160 fact-filled pages
* Each is colourfully illustrated with more than one hundred dramatic photographs, and often with superb technical drawings
* Each contains concisely presented data and accurate descriptions of major international weapons
* Each represents tremendous value

Further titles in this series are in preparation
Your military library will be incomplete without them

PRINTED IN BELGIUM BY
proost
INTERNATIONAL BOOK PRODUCTION